IN THE IMAGE OF GOD

Marriage and Chastity
in Christian Life

August 5, 1984
We greet you dear Arthur
and Yvonne on your
Wedding Day. May it really
be a witness to the
uniting love of Christ
in the Church. We wish
you God's Blessing and
Protection on your Marriage
Bond

your brother and sister
Johann Christoph + Verena

BY THE SAME AUTHOR

Freedom from Sinful Thoughts:
Christ Alone Breaks the Curse, 1973

also available in German

Freiheit von Gedankensünden:
Nur Christus bricht den Fluch

IN THE IMAGE OF GOD

Marriage and Chastity
in Christian Life

by

Heini Arnold

PLOUGH PUBLISHING HOUSE
Hutterian Society of Brothers
Rifton, New York

© 1977 by the Plough Publishing House of
The Woodcrest Service Committee, Inc.
Hutterian Society of Brothers
Rifton, NY 12471
All rights reserved

Library of Congress Cataloging in Publication Data

Arnold, Heini, 1913–
    In the image of God: marriage and chastity in Christian life.

    1. Marriage I. Title.
BV835.A76   234'.165   76–53542
ISBN 0–87486–169–1

Printed at the Plough Press
Hutterian Society of Brothers
Farmington, PA, USA

*Blessed are the pure in heart:
for they shall see God.*
　　　　　　Matthew 5:8

Dedicated to my wife and faithful comrade
Annemarie

CONTENTS

Foreword	xi
Introduction	1
1. Man the Image of God	9
2. Regaining the Image of God	23
3. It Is Not Good for Man to Be Alone	29
4. Man's Way to God	35
5. Every Man Is a Helper	41
6. The First Sin of All	45
7. Different Areas of the Sensuous	51
8. The Sacredness of the Marriage Act	63
9. With or Without God?	71
10. What Is Impurity?	77
11. The Insensuous Person	83
12. The Pure in Heart	91
13. The Sensuous Sphere in Marriage	103
14. Marriage in the Holy Spirit	113
15. The Glory of Purity	125
16. Marriage in the Church	135
17. Especially for Young Couples	143
18. Fatherhood and Motherhood	157
19. The Special Service of the Unmarried and the Widowed	161
Bibliography	167

To the reader

The character of love and marriage is so intimate, so close to the heart of man, so central in man's relationship to God, so holy when sanctioned by God and so dangerous to the soul when not, that we have a special request to the reader not to open these pages without a deep reverence for God.

FOREWORD

This book grew out of a need and a living experience in the communities of the Hutterian Society of Brothers, also known as the Bruderhof Communities. In the year 1974 there were several weddings in the communities. At communal meetings in preparation for these weddings, Heini Arnold, the Elder, spoke about marriage in its deepest sense and also about the special calling of those who remain single. In the course of these talks, partly prepared and partly spoken freely, he drew on thoughts and guidelines from a number of sources, including the writings of his father, Eberhard Arnold; the Hutterian confession of faith written down in the sixteenth century by Peter Rideman; and his own extensive experience over many years in the Bruderhof communities, where many have sought his advice and help. He wishes, however, to acknowledge in a special way his indebtedness to Dietrich von Hildebrand and Friedrich von Gagern, whose books he has found very valuable. (See bibliography.)

Today, when the clear teaching of Jesus and the

apostles about marriage and purity are so desperately needed and so rarely heeded and practiced, we are grateful that Heini Arnold has agreed to the publishing of these talks. We believe they will be as helpful to a wider circle of readers as they are to the members of the Bruderhof communities.

For those who are not familiar with the Hutterian Society of Brothers of today or with the 450-year history of the Brothers known as Hutterians, it may be helpful to tell a little about their background.

In June 1920, a small group of Christians began community life in the little village of Sannerz in Germany. For Eberhard and Emmy Arnold and her sister Else von Hollander, three of the founding members, this was a further step in a long and deep search for a practical life lived only in Jesus, a search which began at the time of Eberhard and Emmy's engagement in 1907. In 1927, after a period of crisis and growth, the group acquired a small farm in the Rhön hills not far from Sannerz. They called their new settlement, initially about thirty adults and children, *Bruderhof,* in memory of the many communal households of the Brothers known as Hutterians in Moravia in the 16th and early 17th centuries. Today, in 1977, this small beginning in Germany has grown to four larger community settlements, over one thousand adults and children in the United States and England.

Foreword

Eberhard Arnold visited the thirty communal colonies of the Hutterian Brothers in the United States and Canada in 1930–1931. During this time he and the little German Bruderhof were received into the full unity of the Hutterian Church. After the death of Eberhard Arnold in 1935, a time of discord, turmoil, and separation followed, especially in the fifties. On January 7, 1974, in Sturgeon Creek Colony, Headingly, Manitoba, unity was reestablished with the more than two hundred Hutterian colonies now existing. We of the Society of Brothers are deeply moved by this event and consider it a gift of God's infinite grace and mercy that forgiveness for past wrongs was granted.

The present Hutterian Society of Brothers is made up of people from all manner of backgrounds who are committed to a life of love as followers of Christ. This commitment means the giving-up of all property and all self-interest. In the daily practical life of the community there is no private enterprise. No individual tries to achieve all he can for himself. Each one gives his time, work, and possessions to the community, which then takes care of the necessities of life. We strive for a real working together in the Spirit whether in building and maintenance, office, school, kitchen, laundry, the Community Playthings workshop, or other work. Each guest, like each member, gives himself to be used where the Church community needs his work.

The beginning of our publishing work goes back to the time before the community started and was established to spread the challenge of an uncompromising commitment to Jesus. This is still our aim today as the Plough Publishing House, and to anyone who is interested we will gladly send a catalog.

The family is the important unit within the community; but each family belongs firstly to God, secondly to His Church, and lastly to one another. Parents live with their children in small family apartments and are responsible for the bringing-up of their children in the love of God, working closely with the community in this.

Brothers and sisters stand in great reverence before the gift of new life to the community. Mother and baby are at home for about six weeks, after which the baby enters the baby house for part of the day and the mother returns to the communal work. The mother's work hours allow her time for the personal care of her child. Children are together by age, moving through the baby house, kindergarten, and elementary school, staffed by our own brothers and sisters. We regard these early years of childhood as precious years in which we can receive from the child a feeling of his closeness to God and in which our task is to protect his true childlikeness.

Foreword

The Bruderhof is not a retreat from the world. It is a place where members and guests have to take an attitude to the many influences that destroy a Christian life—lying, militarism, impurity, and self-seeking. No resolutions of human will, no matter how sincere, are strong enough to overcome these influences. Only through a deep love for Jesus can they be overcome. It is our conviction that community life must be firmly founded on *Jesus* and not on economic, social, or even religious idealism. People the world over are willing to work and make sacrifices for personal goals. The brotherly life asks even more: openness to purity and truth and love and poverty, to full fellowship in the Spirit, and to the justice of God's coming Kingdom.

Anyone who wants insight into our common life will be welcome to visit if he is open and seeking. We neither charge guests for accommodation nor pay them for their work. Because of the number of guests who come to us, please write in advance if you wish to visit one of our communities of the Hutterian Society of Brothers:

Woodcrest, Rifton, New York 12471
New Meadow Run, Farmington, Pennsylvania 15437
Deer Spring, Norfolk, Connecticut 06058
Darvell, Robertsbridge, Sussex, England TN32 5DR

The Editors

INTRODUCTION

With the publishing of this little book I want to express my longing that it might point engaged and married couples to Jesus.[1] There is a deep connection between marriage and Jesus. It is not without significance that Jesus changed water into wine at a wedding. He loved the people at the wedding feast in Cana.

We are called to think deeply about the meaning of marriage in this day and age. Marriage is a gift from God. It means that one man and one woman become one. Peter Rideman points out clearly that true marriage consists of three grades:

> Marriage is a union of two, in which one takes the other to care for and the second submitteth to obey the first, and thus through their agreement two become one, and are no longer two but one. But if this is to be done in a godly way they must come together not through their own action and

---

[1] Not all of this book is suitable for reading in public since I have tried to speak openly to the young people of our corrupt time. The reader should use his discretion in choosing suitable material for meetings.

choice, but in accordance with God's will and order, and therefore neither leave nor forsake the other but suffer both ill and good together all their days. Marriage is, however, in three grades or steps. First is that of God with the soul or spirit of man, then that of the spirit with the body, and thirdly that of one body with another, that is, the marriage of man with woman.[1]

Eberhard Arnold enlarges on this in his book *Love and Marriage in the Spirit*:

> First is the marriage of God to His people; the marriage of Christ to His Church; the marriage of God's Spirit to the spirit of man.
>
> Second is the justice of God's people among themselves; the fellowship within the Church, the members of the Body of Christ forming a complete unity; the fellowship of spirit and soul.
>
> Third is the unity between one man and one woman. This unity is not the first grade of unity; it is not unity proper. "It is the last unity—visible, understandable, and recognizable by all."[2]

This bond of marriage, which begins with two being of one spirit, is taken so seriously by Jesus that He calls even a glance, a lustful glance toward another woman, adultery in the heart. We can see from this

---

[1] Peter Rideman, *Confession of Faith: Account of Our Religion, Doctrine, and Faith,* 2nd ed. (Rifton, NY: Plough Publishing House, 1970), pp. 97–98.

[2] Eberhard Arnold, *Love and Marriage in the Spirit* (Rifton, NY: Plough Publishing House, 1965), pp. 118–119.

Introduction

sharpness what a horror adultery is in the eyes of God. The whole Bible protests against it. Even the worship of idols by the children of Israel is called adultery.

Marriage then is the bond between one man and one woman in which they are of one soul. It is possible to be of one spirit with every brother and sister in the Church. It is also possible to be of one heart and soul with them, and that is how it should be. But there is a difference beween an engaged or married couple and others: there is a special love between these two people. Their hearts feel a special joy when the beloved one is near. Even when the whole Church becomes of one heart and one soul, it is something quite specific when two love one another in a special way and want to be faithful to one another and keep their relationship pure. This is God's will, and there is His special blessing on it. God leads the two together.

We can see from the engagement letters of my parents, Eberhard and Emmy Arnold, that the strong call to be of one spirit was of first importance with them: Jesus was everything.[1] But they were also of one heart and soul. They felt the purely human

[1] Eberhard and Emmy Arnold, *Seeking for the Kingdom of God: Origins of the Bruderhof Communities,* ed. Heini and Annemarie Arnold (Rifton, NY: Plough Publishing House, 1974).

joy and human sorrow—joy in meeting, sorrow in separating—like anyone else.

Now certainly, marriage is a physical union in which one man and one woman become one flesh, as Jesus expresses it. If that is broken by the sin of adultery, it is terrible in the eyes of God. By that sin the unity of one spirit and one soul—of everything—is broken and smashed. Nothing is left except the hope that through repentance and God's grace and forgiveness something new will be given. The old bond does not exist anymore. It is broken.

The early Church took marriage extremely seriously, just as Jesus did. The blessing of God is on a marriage if it represents *first* the unity of spirit, heart, and soul, and *then* the physical unity: not the physical unity *first,* then perhaps a little unity of heart and soul and a very little unity of spirit. The blessing of God is on any couple, young or old, who are united in the Spirit of Jesus and the fear of God, and who experience unity in the right order. But there is a curse of God on adultery, on destroying this wonderful gift. What was first a blessing for two people then becomes a curse. There is no excuse for it, especially not for anyone who believes in Jesus.

Peter Rideman writes the following about baptized members of the Church who fall into the terrible sin of adultery (I mean full adultery, becoming one flesh with another):

Introduction

> The Lord Christ saith concerning adultery, "Whosoever looketh on a woman to lust after her hath committed adultery with her already in his heart."[1]

These sharp and serious words should show us how much joy God has in the unity of two people and how even the slightest damage to it falls under God's strict judgment. Peter Rideman continues:

> Thirdly, there cometh adultery with the work of the flesh, if one or the other of the partners in marriage go to another man or woman. Where this taketh place, where one committeth adultery in this way, the other should put him or her away and have no more in common with him or her before he or she hath shown real fruits of repentance. For where one mixeth with the transgressor before he or she hath repented, one committeth adultery with the other, even though they were husband and wife before. For it is no longer a marriage, because it is broken until through repentance it is healed, therefore this should be punished by separation as much as the other.

This means that if the adultery committed by one partner is known to the other, and still the married partners become one flesh, this latter act is to be treated as adultery and the two should be separated from the Church or excluded.

[1] Peter Rideman, *Confession of Faith,* p. 102.

The parable of the Ten Virgins should be a warning and a challenge to all of us because Jesus again and again compares His coming to a wedding feast in the Kingdom of Heaven. Marriage points to the coming of Jesus: the virgins await the Bridegroom. *All ten* virgins are preparing to meet their Bridegroom. He is not speaking about the world on the one hand and the Church on the other. He is challenging the Church.

> Then shall the kingdom of heaven be likened unto ten virgins, which took their lamps, and went forth to meet the bridegroom.
>
> And five of them were wise, and five were foolish.
>
> They that were foolish took their lamps, and took no oil with them:
>
> But the wise took oil in their vessels with their lamps.
>
> While the bridegroom tarried, they all slumbered and slept.
>
> And at midnight there was a cry made, Behold, the bridegroom cometh; go ye out to meet him.
>
> Then all those virgins arose, and trimmed their lamps.
>
> And the foolish said unto the wise, Give us of your oil; for our lamps are gone out.
>
> But the wise answered, saying, Not so; lest there be not enough for us and you: but go ye rather to them that sell, and buy for yourselves.

And while they went to buy, the bridegroom came; and they that were ready went in with him to the marriage: and the door was shut.

Afterward came also the other virgins, saying, Lord, Lord, open to us.

But he answered and said, Verily I say unto you, I know you not.

Watch therefore, for ye know neither the day nor the hour wherein the Son of man cometh.

(Matt. 25:1–13)

Heini Arnold

1. MAN THE IMAGE OF GOD

Then God said, "Let us make man in our image and likeness to rule the fish in the sea, the birds of heaven, the cattle, all wild animals on earth, and all reptiles that crawl upon the earth." So God created man in his own image; in the image of God he created him; male and female he created them. God blessed them and said to them, "Be fruitful and increase, fill the earth and subdue it, rule over the fish in the sea, the birds of heaven, and every living thing that moves upon the earth." God also said, "I give you all plants that bear seed everywhere on earth, and every tree bearing fruit which yields seed: they shall be yours for food. All green plants I give for food to the wild animals, to all the birds of heaven, and to all reptiles on earth, every living creature." So it was; and God saw all that he had made, and it was very good. Evening came, and morning came, a sixth day.
(Gen. 1:26–31, NEB)
Then the Lord God said, "It is not good for the man to be alone. I will provide a partner for him." So God formed out of the ground all the wild

animals and all the birds of heaven. He brought them to the man to see what he would call them, and whatever the man called each living creature, that was its name. Thus the man gave names to all cattle, to the birds of heaven, and to every wild animal; but for the man himself no partner had yet been found. And so the Lord God put the man into a trance, and while he slept, he took one of his ribs and closed the flesh over the place. The Lord God then built up the rib, which he had taken out of the man, into a woman. He brought her to the man, and the man said:

> "Now this, at last—
> bone from my bones,
> flesh from my flesh!—
> this shall be called woman,
> for from man was this taken."

That is why a man leaves his father and mother and is united to his wife, and the two become one flesh. Now they were both naked, the man and his wife, but they had no feeling of shame toward one another. (Gen. 2:18–25, NEB)

The serpent was more crafty than any wild creature that the Lord God had made. He said to the woman, "Is it true that God has forbidden you to eat from any tree in the garden?" The woman answered the serpent, "We may eat the fruit of any tree in the garden, except for the tree in the middle of the garden; God has forbidden us either to eat or to touch the fruit of that; if we do, we shall die." The serpent said, "Of course you will not die. God knows that as soon as you eat it, your eyes will be opened and you will be like gods knowing both good and evil." When the woman saw that the fruit of the tree was good to eat, and that it was pleasing to the eye and tempting to contemplate, she took some and ate it. She also gave her husband some and he ate it. Then the eyes of both of them were opened and they discovered that they were naked; so they stitched fig-leaves together and made themselves loincloths.

The man and his wife heard the sound of the Lord God walking in the garden at the time of the evening breeze and hid from the Lord God among the trees of the garden. But the Lord God called to the man and said to him, "Where are you?" He replied, "I heard the sound as you were walking in the garden, and I was afraid because I was naked, and I hid myself." God answered, "Who told you that you were naked? Have you eaten from the tree which I forbade you?" The man said, "The woman you gave me for a companion, she gave me fruit from the tree and I ate it." Then the Lord God said to the woman, "What is this that you have done?" The woman said, "The serpent tricked me, and I ate."

(Gen. 3:1–13, NEB)

If with due reverence we regard man as the image of God, then there must be some likeness to God in man, the created being. We cannot simply reject the assumption that in God there are both: what we as His creatures know as the masculine and the feminine. Everything God creates gives us an insight into His nature. It lives in Him, therefore He created it.

All we know is a fallen creation. Therefore, although God can definitely be recognized and experienced in creation and in nature, so gloriously beautiful, what we find there is not only God. The same is true in the picture of bride and bridegroom and of marriage. When God created Adam, He said that everything He had made was good. But God saw that it would not be good for man to remain alone. Therefore He took a rib from Adam and from it created woman. Thus woman, too, was an image of God. The story of the rib may be a parable in the same way as the Bible is full of parables. But I believe one thing is true: God first created Adam, and it was good; in Adam there were both the masculine and the feminine. (I do not want this to be taken in a theological, much less biological sense.) God then set apart almost everything that was feminine in man and created a virgin, who thus was an image of God too and a companion to Adam.

I do not believe that the difference between man and woman is an absolute one. In a true woman there is often courageous manliness, and in a true man there is usually also something truly motherly. Jesus, the only true man, was not ashamed to apply to Himself the motherly picture of the hen longing to gather her chickens.

In this sinful and corrupt generation, the difference between man and woman, between boy and girl, is being blurred and distorted. These are signs of demonic impurity that destroy the image of God. When I say that in God there must be both the masculine and the feminine because both, man and woman, are in God's image, I would like to be sure that this is taken with very great reverence. To think of these things in an irreverent way would be very wrong. Let us look at the creation on our earth: mighty mountains, immense oceans, rivers and great expanses of water, storms, thunder and lightning, huge icebergs; and then look at a meadow sprinkled with the most delicate flowers, as though devised by a virgin. Perhaps the best way to describe it is by saying that what is specifically manly is patterned after God, is an image of God, and so is what is specifically womanly—gentle motherliness and a sensitivity toward the coarseness of the world.

Let us look at our world again: forests, meadows, birds, deer, a valley in the moonlight, a sunset, the starlit heavens. When we think of the starry heavens, the question arises: could God really be so materialistic as to have created so much visible life just here on this little speck of dust we call earth, leaving everything else absolutely dead? Anyone who thinks deeply will find this impossible; and I am absolutely convinced that, just as this earth has an Earth-Spirit, a Prince of this World, so each star has an angel, a spiritual prince or spiritual authority who animates and rules over it. The sun has a fire-angel; the millions of suns in the universe have fire-angels. We have no knowledge of the beauty of the angel-world; very few have seen it. But if we had the possibility of experiencing the star-worlds with their angels or spiritual authorities and princes, I think we would be amazed how wonderfully tender God's creation is, with the tenderness of virginity, and yet how wonderfully powerful and manly. In the New Testament the person to whom an angel appears is often greatly frightened, and the angel's first words are: "Do not fear!" This is what Gabriel said when he came to Mary; this is what the angels said when they appeared to the shepherds in the field; this is what happened at the resurrection. Angels are sometimes described as shining, radiant youths dressed in white, as for instance in the accounts of the resurrection and ascension.

> Suddenly there was a violent earthquake; an angel of the Lord descended from heaven; he came to the stone and rolled it away, and sat himself down on it. His face shone like lightning; his garments

were white as snow. At the sight of him the guards shook with fear and lay like the dead.

(Matt. 28:2–4, NEB)

They went into the tomb, where they saw a youth sitting on the right-hand side, wearing a white robe; and they were dumbfounded.

(Mark 16:5, NEB)

While they stood utterly at a loss, all of a sudden two men in dazzling garments were at their side.

(Luke 24:4, NEB)

As she wept, she peered into the tomb; and she saw two angels in white sitting there, one at the head, and one at the feet, where the body of Jesus had lain. (John 20:12, NEB)

As he was going, and as they were gazing intently into the sky, all at once there stood beside them two men in white who said, 'Men of Galilee, why stand there looking up into the sky?' (Acts 1:10, NEB)

We just cannot imagine the infinite beauty there is in God's creation. The beauty of it is often overwhelming. It is a sign to us that God's creation holds beauty upon beauty hidden within it, which will be fully revealed one day in God's heavenly Realm, in God's Paradise, in God's Kingdom.

For those who have not read my pamphlet *Man the Image of God and Modern Psychology,* I would like to say a few words about the theory of evolution.[1]

[1] Heini Arnold, *Man the Image of God and Modern Psychology* (Rifton, NY: Plough Publishing House, 1973).

As far as scholars know, it is impossible to prove that the world was created in seven days, and therefore it is also impossible to prove that man was created in one day. According to Darwin's teaching, man evolved from the primitive cell to an ape-like creature and from this creature to man. I believe that in this respect science is right in saying that the Bible should not be taken literally, and I think we should take into consideration that for God a very long time can be as a day, and a day can be a very long time—it is not just twenty-four hours. How man was created may well remain a mystery for God alone to unveil. When we see on occasion a wholly genuine, free, and natural person, who is filled with the Spirit of God, we sense something of the nature of God's image. We can experience the same thing with a child when in a very special moment he talks about God from the depths of his heart. I think it is out of the question that man should have evolved, without a special act of intervention from God, from the first cell through the ape-like stage to man as we know him today. And it was on that day and in that hour when He intervened that God created Adam, and on that day and in that hour that God created Eve.

No matter at what stage of evolution this creature was that then became man, God breathed His breath into it and formed it in its inner potentials into an

Clarification

I believe in the Word of the Bible, and I think we do not have the right to change anything in it. I was thinking of the words of the Second Letter of Peter, chapter 3, verse 8, when I wrote, "I believe that in this respect science is right in saying that the Bible should not be taken literally." Peter writes: "With the Lord one day is like a thousand years and a thousand years like one day."

I do not believe in Darwin's theory of evolution. I believe that God breathed His breath into man (Genesis 2:7): "Then the Lord God formed a man from the dust of the ground and breathed into his nostrils the breath of life. Thus the man became a living creature."

Darwin's whole theory of evolution is not God-centered, and therefore it is dangerous to faith. Only when we look at creation in a God-centered way will all things fall into place.

Where would man be if God had not breathed His breath into him?

January 1977 *Heini Arnold*

image of God. It has not yet been revealed to us, I believe, what potentials for wonderful experiences are given to man. It must have been an unbelievable religious experience for this first man when, coming from the animal world, he suddenly experienced God—we men seldom experience God like that, breathing His living breath into us and speaking directly to our hearts. Yet the same thing happened to Mary. So I do not see that any great problem arises between the story of creation in the Bible and theories of evolution. (But by that I do not mean that I agree with all the ideas in these theories.)

What is man? He exists in a field of tension between animal and spirit. Most people do not recognize this all-important tension. They ignore the fact that they are called to something higher than being an animal, that they should allow the Spirit to live in them. Many people cannot find a relationship to themselves. Von Gagern calls this not-finding-of-oneself the real neurosis or mental sickness of our time.[1] The German language uses the expression *geisteskrank,* sick in spirit. Just at the present time this sickness is widespread among those men in whom the picture of man as the image of God has been lost.

---

[1] Friedrich E. Freiherr v. Gagern, *Der Mensch als Bild: Beiträge zur Anthropologie,* 2nd ed. (Frankfurt am Main: Verlag Josef Knecht, 1955), p. 14.

While there is truth in von Gagern's words that the cause of all mental sickness lies in this not-finding-of-oneself, I believe that there is no healing of the human spirit or the human soul without a direct relationship to our Father in Heaven, to God the Creator. Jesus is the only way to the Father, to the Creator. At the Cross we find God, we find our own calling. We find healing because we find God, and in God we are able to find ourselves. Through this our spirit is healed. At the Cross there is healing for all men. Through this healing, man can live from a true and genuine heart. He becomes a child again. Christ, the only example of a human being who is free from all contradictions within himself, can heal people. Apart from Christ, in everyone a neurotic attitude is to a greater or lesser extent inborn. The extreme case of this attitude is a complete inability to find oneself, which is complete derangement.

At the beginning of these pages, man is described as a being created by God, founded on God. I am referring to the story of creation. When a person is severely mentally sick, one might even describe him as a man without God. Mental illness is an abnormal inner attitude toward God, toward fellow human beings, and toward one's own self. To feel that one is without God is not a proof of ungodliness. It is an accepted fact that many serious Christians have suffered severe inner pain because they often felt they were without God for prolonged periods of time. On the Cross, Christ himself had to experience this state of darkness, a darkness so terrible that we men cannot comprehend it. This is expressed in His words: My God, my God, why hast Thou forsaken me?

How can a thinking person ever find a real trust for his existence as long as he traces his origins back solely to a void or to chaos, to a primeval slime or to an ape-like state, as long as he feels like jetsam blindly thrown up, and as long as he has before his eyes the complete disintegration of his existence at the end of his sojourn on this earth? In this we can see that neither man's spirit nor his heart and soul can find healing without God.

However, we have to be on our guard against arrogance in man. Every believer has to take care that he himself does not fall into the sin of arrogance or self-glorification. The man who glorifies himself, who does not have a living faith, is on his way to meet a dreadful fate.

The man who denies that God is his origin, who denies that God is the living reality in his life, will also lose a healthy attitude toward himself. This man's deepest heart gets buried under his ego. That is why we find such a terrible emptiness and such terrible need wherever there is a deeply rooted self-idolatry, whether conscious or unconscious. There are some young people who are really looking for the truth, but their self-idolatry brings with it a contempt for the worth and dignity of other people. At its worst, this means that another person does not count anymore if he is not useful; man is seen only in the light of usefulness. As soon as we evaluate another man in the light of his usefulness, and not as God sees him, we are cut off from our *own* inner worth and our *own* inner life. The fear of being nothing is actually the fear for his existence exhibited by the self-glorifying man, the man without God.

How unhappy and neurotic are men without God! One could say a lot about our time: government officials have been caught in their own web of lies; in high schools and colleges, in public and private life so much is unhealthy. And the Churches have very little, if anything, to say. I am speaking here about the young people. They are plagued by impure, lying spirits. They try to obliterate the difference between man and woman. They try to disregard God's creation. Yet we cannot redeem ourselves; we are God's creatures, and we can find healing only if we believe that God has created us. But we have to understand one thing clearly, that there is no way to God the Father in Heaven except through Jesus Christ. Accordingly, faith in God the Creator, from

Man the Image of God

whom man has his existence, and in Jesus Christ is a necessary prerequisite for mental health, for a man's finding of his true self, and for self-realization.

What is said above about finding oneself and self-realization can of course be completely misunderstood to mean that man is placed in the center of the universe. This would actually be contrary to his real self and his self-realization. We have to find Jesus on the Cross. We have to experience God the Creator in such a way that we know ourselves to be created by Him and in this way find a relationship to Him. If the only center we can find is our ego, the final result will be insanity. Healing begins as soon as a person finds the "thou." The "thou" in another person protects us from complete insanity. In Jesus Christ alone is complete light. In Him we find the "Thou" which heals the soul and the heart and which leads to the "thou" in a human being. It is a matter of a personal encounter with Jesus in our hearts. No matter where we are on earth, such an encounter leads us to brothers and sisters. To experience the "Thou" in Jesus leads us to love our fellowmen. A person who has experienced Jesus as the "Thou" will try to find community in Christ.

2. REGAINING THE IMAGE OF GOD

That man is a creature dependent on God and has his origin in God becomes especially clear to us when we meet a man who reflects the image of God in a special way: an image of Him who is all love and yet at the same time is strict, who judges justly and yet at the same time is the understanding Father, who is strict where there is evil and yet at the same time is gentleness, truthfulness, absolute goodness, and perfect beauty. This is true also for the virgin and the woman. When she has the purity of true womanliness—is really chaste—we say of her: this is a true virgin or this is a true woman. The same is true of motherliness.

There are situations in which the nature of God's image is put before our eyes in a special way and the difference between man and woman is very relative. Such a situation is martyrdom, suffering for the sake of Jesus. In the time of the early Christians as well as in the Reformation times of the Anabaptists and early Hutterian Brothers,[1] there were men who truly reflected the image of God in this way. There were also women and girls who were just as courageous and ready to suffer and even die for truth's sake as the men were. Also here we see the nature of God's image. From these examples we can conclude that within man there lives an image of true man which bears a likeness to the image of God.

Man has a strong sense of what is in the image of God. When a man is both upright and kind, when he radiates goodness, when he radiates love to children, when he has an inner beauty all his own, we would regard him as truly "human." When we meet this man who radiates only Jesus, our hearts rejoice, also the hearts of those who do not yet believe in Jesus. I experienced this very forcefully in my childhood and youth with my father. Unfortunately this Jesus-likeness very often brings out an amazing hatred from some people. Others admire such a man as if he were a super-human being or a god. This is one tragic sign of our superficial day and age. A true Christian rejects all such praise. He

---

[1] See the article by Eberhard Arnold, "The Hutterian Brothers: Four Centuries of Common Life and Work," in Peter Rideman, *Confession of Faith,* pp. 273–295.

Regaining the Image of God

knows that everything is given through grace alone. He points to Christ.

Where these human or natural virtues that let God's nature shine through are lacking in a man, we would say he is inhuman. He may be a man who is hardhearted and ruled by the dollar, who has no justice within him, who recklessly decides the fate of other men and tramples on them in order to rise and become rich; or he may be a man who seeks spiritual power over others, which is soul-killing. Many years ago, on one of my fund-raising trips for the hospital we used to have in Paraguay, I met a man who had started out as a poverty-stricken child and become rich, and there he sat now with his millions. I asked him for help and was given a few dollars; later I heard that this man not only despised his fellowmen but actually trampled them underfoot for the sake of money. It is at least as evil if a man (or a woman) misuses his fellowmen's inner dedication to Jesus to trample on their souls so as to rise to spiritual power and recognition. This spiritual ambition is one of the greatest enemies of Christ. It reveals something of the Antichrist.

Let us never forget that we men have fallen away from God and have lost this reflection of the image of God to a high degree. There is, however, a possibility of finding the image of God in man again. It can be given through repentance, conversion, and faith. What happened at Pentecost when the Holy Spirit, the true Physician of hearts, was poured out over the people and they cried out, "What shall we do?" Peter answered, "Repent and be baptized, every one of you, in the name of Jesus the Messiah for the forgiveness of your sins." "In these and many other words he pressed his case and pleaded with them: 'Save yourselves', he said, 'from this crooked age.'" (Acts 2:38, 40, NEB)

If man were completely evil and corrupt through and through before being born again of the Holy Spirit, there would be neither room for the divine image nor the possibility of stirring his conscience. The fact that we human beings do have consciences that can and will be moved puts us on a level above all other creatures on this earth. Man is an image, an image of God, a reflection of the primary Source. In the word "image of God" lies the greatness of being human, something which is almost unfathomable and remains a mystery we cannot grasp. We should find an inner vision and an inner reverence for this fact that man is an image of God, seeing with what devotion he opens up to love and with what wonder he submerges himself in streams of holiness.

The most significant sign of man being made in God's image is man's heart. How deeply and wonderfully the human heart can grasp and understand! Only too often we men unfortunately tend toward the

Regaining the Image of God

superficial, sensuous sphere and thereby miss the might and power of all that comes from God and that we *could* experience. Later on we will speak more about the meaning and danger of sensuousness. To this sensuousness belongs everything that is outwardly human: the eyes, the ears, eating and drinking, and also sexual attraction between boys and girls and between men and women. If we let this sensuous sphere rule us, we miss the wonderful possibility the human heart has of experiencing the greatest of all things. Many people have no idea what potential their heart has for such great experiences. Whoever wants to go the way that leads to the wonderful experiencing of the image of God should start at the stable in Bethlehem and end at the Cross. At the Cross we find more than the image of God. We find God in the form of a man. In this ultimate depth a bride and bridegroom can experience Eternity together at their wedding.

3. IT IS NOT GOOD FOR MAN TO BE ALONE

Then the Lord God said, 'It is not good for the man to be alone. I will provide a partner for him.'
(Gen. 2:18, NEB)

There is little that is so difficult for a person to bear as loneliness. What a help it is for a prisoner in solitary confinement to share his prison cell even with a spider! At least *something* living! Without the animals on his island, Robinson Crusoe would not only have starved but would also have become insane. Man is a communal being. Yet the world today is frighteningly uncommunal and unjust. I believe in my heart that being separated and cut off from God and man leads to complete insanity.

Man's instinctive longing to achieve greater and greater likeness to God urges him to community. So it is also between man and woman in marriage. In engagement and marriage both man and woman are set free from their onesidedness. When a person encounters love in the other, he must first become a true man. This is especially true for a young couple.

But basically all men should be brothers and sisters. For that reason it is natural for us to help one another to become true men.

In His farewell speech and in His last prayer (recorded in the Gospel of John), Jesus points out how terribly deep the need for inner community is within mankind. This is true for all men, but especially for a bride and bridegroom. Jesus makes it clear that we cannot follow Him in solitude. A hermit who has cut himself off from all mankind cannot be a Christian. So Jesus says:

> 'Dwell in me, as I in you. No branch can bear fruit by itself, but only if it remains united with the vine; no more can you bear fruit, unless you remain united with me.
>
> 'I am the vine, and you the branches. He who dwells in me, as I dwell in him, bears much fruit; for apart from me you can do nothing.'
>
> (John 15:4, 5, NEB)

Nothing I can say to engaged couples can surpass these words. If you isolate yourselves inwardly from each other, nothing will go well. And if you stay on the branch as a family clique without union with Jesus, your life will be fruitless, and you will be in danger of losing eternal life. This is the mystery of Christ's Body. We love one another. We also love those who have gone before us long ago. But above

It Is Not Good for Man to Be Alone

all, we love the Vine, Christ himself, who is our support, our hope, and our life.

So marriage is not the highest goal of the community for which God has created man. Since the time of Jesus there have been many who have renounced marriage in order to live for the highest goal. Think of the Apostle Paul or Francis of Assisi and his brothers, who were kindled by the Holy Spirit. Our beloved Jesus points to the very depths before the crucifixion:

> 'I give you a new commandment: love one another; as I have loved you, so you are to love one another. If there is this love among you, then all will know that you are my disciples.'
> (John 13:34, 35, NEB)

In John, chapter 17, is the most heartfelt prayer that has ever been recorded:

> 'But it is not for these alone that I pray, but for those also who through their words put their faith in me; may they all be one: as thou, Father, art in me, and I in thee, so also may they be in us, that the world may believe that thou didst send me.'
> (John 17:20, 21, NEB)

In marriage, the husband should lead his wife to God; he is given to her as a helper in God's stead. So too, the wife is given to her husband as a helper in God's stead. Later on, if children are given, the children should honor their father and mother in

God's stead. In order to be real fathers and real mothers, the parents have to be human beings in the truest sense.

Love is man's calling. How is he to develop his love fully if not toward the "thou" of another person? This is true in a special way for an engaged or married couple. But there is no doubt whatever that it is God's will for every human to be the "thou" for every other human being. Every man is called to be his brother's helper in God's stead. Anyone who is filled with the fullness of God's love can never be lonely and withdrawn, like a hermit. For every Christian, the people he meets are the objects of his love; he loves them because in them, even in the least of his brothers, he loves God. In this way the "thou" in our fellowman does indeed attain the significance of being a helper in God's stead. Man's life is then fulfilled: through his fellowman his love is kindled and proved and brought to fruition. The word "helper" often refers to God himself; yet Jesus does give us the task of helping our brother, of leading him to God so that in God he can find the perfect help.

There is no doubt that when a person meets his brother's inmost heart he can help him in God's stead. We know that all this help can in fact be given by God himself, but God wants men to find community with one another and to help one another in love.

It Is Not Good for Man to Be Alone

To be allowed to be a helping "thou" to another in God's stead—what dignity, what an overwhelming gift, what an obligation, and what a task! And so all engaged and married couples, too, have the task of helping each other in God's stead, each in his or her own way. The husband is meant to lead his wife to what is good and to lead her to Christ. The wife is meant to be her husband's helper. How great these tasks are! And if children are given as well and the task consists also of being a real father and a real mother, this is something truly tremendous and splendid. Father and mother should be images of God so that they can show their children the way to God.

Man stands in the place of God toward other men. How are two people to help each other as friends, let alone truly love each other as an engaged or married couple, unless God's love is awakened by the wind of the Spirit even when they are not aware of it? Let us compare man's inner life to King David's harp: the wind plays across the strings calling forth the deepest feelings of heart and soul.[1] The Spirit awakens the love to God and the love between two. Is it not bliss when two people find each other and want to love each other in God? God and blissfulness are then the same. God is the Giver of all true bliss.

---

[1] According to Rabbinic records, King David was fond of hanging his harp where the night breezes could blow over the strings, making harmonious sounds.

4. MAN'S WAY TO GOD

In the "thou" as representative of God and through this "thou," the Christian loves God, who is behind everything, who shines through the transparent "thou." We experience in Jesus that, in marriage, only what is divine in a human being endures and is worthy of love. The "thou" between bride and bridegroom is a great grace. It has a redeeming and softening effect that can release man from his ego and from the deathly sickness of this ego.

The redemptive effect of this "thou" from bridegroom to bride, however, can never be complete in itself. To begin with, we are all burdened by guilt, and a bridegroom cannot solve the need of a burdened conscience for his bride. Nor can a bride do this for her bridegroom. Full redemption can be found only in Jesus. Jesus opens up the way to God's heart. Here is perfect love, here is perfect freedom. Everything that is stone hard in a sinful and isolated heart softens and grows warm through Him before whom all coldness of heart has to yield.

For the Christian, therefore, there is no such thing as loneliness. God is always near. A true Christian always finds someone to love. As long as a person suffers from loneliness, he desires only to *be* loved; he does not seek the happiness, the much greater happiness, of loving another. God comes to meet us in our inner being if we seek this community, and therewith He comes to meet us in every human being. Every person becomes a brother or a sister. Unless we acknowledge that in us which is of God—that which requires community—we are truly lonely. Then we must try to open our senses and our seeking hearts in the right way and ask God to free our choked-up hearts for true, divine love. This can happen only at the Cross.

If anyone should complain that for him God is not living, then more than ever he really must seek. He must look within himself more truly, more deeply. He should not probe into his own heart in a distrustful, critical, and cold way. We read: Anyone who seeks will find; to anyone who knocks, the door will be opened. If a person takes up a different attitude toward himself—a kindlier and more honest attitude—then God will become living for him.

Stronger than any human relationship is the basic relationship of man to God, of which all other relationships are merely likenesses or parables. Ultimately we stand before God. We should be God-fearing, but we will never be afraid of God if we live in the love of God. This shows most plainly when a person faces death. Anyone who has been at the bedside of a dying person knows how absolute in its significance, or in other words how really final, is man's inner relationship to God and his original bond with God; he knows that in the end, when the last breaths are drawn, this relationship to God is the *only* thing that counts.

Certainly we know from the Gospel that love to God can *not* be separated from love to one's neighbor. We must never forget that we cannot find a relationship to God as long as we disregard our fellowman. Man's way to God is through his brother; in marriage, the way to God goes through one's partner. It is in no way advisable to try to find a private relationship to God in order to be accepted by Him in the last hour of life. I have experienced myself at deathbeds that if a man lives completely for his fellowmen as Jesus showed us by His living example, then God will be very close in the last hour too.

How often it happens that a person in need comes with pleading eyes that seem to be asking, "How can you help me? What is my need? How can I find new joy and forget my pain?" Many people suffer under great depression; their question is, "How can

I overcome my depression and all that burdens me? Can you help me carry it?"

If I really love someone, I will be interested to know what there is latent in him, how he will develop. If these questions are really in a man's heart, they will help him to emerge from a self-centered attitude and seek his neighbor. Then there is the possibility of a full awakening, first toward one's neighbor and then toward God. Whoever is really seeking will in some way be found by God. I believe it is very important for every man to recognize that, because he is in the image of God, he can have such experiences of the heart as we can scarcely imagine. The experience of an engagement and a wedding is already a deep one. But most of us have no conception of what God has prepared for all who love and honor Him. We do not know what we *can* experience, and for that reason we do not seek it. I believe that some of us live too much in the world of the senses—in sleeping, in eating and drinking—without searching for the deeper speaking of the heart.

Quite especially in marriage there are different levels of experience. The first is the deep experience of being one heart and soul in the Holy Spirit which, when one finds it, is the most wonderful gift of all. In this experience we have community with all believers of all centuries. The second is the love from heart to heart given especially to two people; their love for one another is so strong that the one, so to speak, hears the heartbeat of the other. The third is the material and physical expression of unity given when two bodies are fused in perfect union, of which Jesus says that man and wife become one flesh.

In his need for complementation, man is nowhere more dependent on another person than in marriage. It can be seen at its clearest in the sexual relationship between man and wife. In that union, that becoming one flesh, a transformation takes place in both so that out of the "I" and the "thou" a new being emerges: the "we." Through the marriage partnership, when man and wife are fused one with the other, something else takes place which may show even in their features. Often the man only attains true manhood through his wife, and the woman only attains true womanhood through her husband.

None of God's commandments are laid upon man by an alien will; they are not laws and commands opposed to man's own nature; rather they are in keeping with that part of human nature created in the image of God and therefore well founded. The more man lives up to the image of God in which he is created, the more strongly does he sense that God's commandments are fitting for him. But the more he betrays and destroys the image of God in himself, the more God's will appears to him as something alien, a moral compulsion that crushes his heart. If we look at the story of the creation, before God's command "Be fruitful" stands His blessing, which gives its character to the whole act of God in giving man a partner. "See, this is my gift to you," God is saying, "This lives in you."

And here I return to my own special theme and repeat, "This lives in you." In every man live almost undreamed-of possibilities of becoming a true man in the image of God. We are too easily satisfied with our daily work, with sleeping, eating, drinking, and with the fact that we are allowed to live in brotherhood. I do not mean this as a reproach; I only want to draw our attention to the fact that God's will is great and He has great things in store for His children. You have to know that something lives in you with possibilities of endless depths, something of which you are as yet perhaps quite unaware. To be fruitful *for* each other by complementing each other; and to be fruitful *with* each other for the preservation of the human race—for these purposes is marriage blessed. Therefore marriage is a joy in Heaven.

5. EVERY MAN IS A HELPER

Every man tries—or at least should try—to find God his Creator and to help his fellowmen. This is his calling as a true man. When we read the story of the creation (especially where it describes how woman was created), we can very well conclude that the essential task for which man and woman were created is to help, to support, to be a friend: it is after all a matter of complementing each other.

Because man is made in the image of God, in His likeness, and because Jesus Christ is the Mediator, the One through whom we have access to the Father, man reflects God also as "mediator," as helper. When Christ lived on the earth, He was a weak man. Today Jesus Christ is Lord. From the Father He has received power to rule over all angels, all stars, all principalities and authorities in the visible and invisible world, over the earth, and over all men. Through the Holy Spirit, the Physician of the heart, man is also given *in Jesus* a wonderful example of a helper. Jesus has the authority to pour out the Holy Spirit. The Holy Spirit brings Christ to us. His name is Comforter, the One who is called upon to help. Perhaps the best translation would be: the Friend. If we describe the Holy Spirit as a friend, then in His capacity as a friend and helper He is the tool of Jesus Christ. Christ does not come to us without the Holy Spirit. In Christ we become holy and firmly grounded helpers of each other in marriage and helpers of our brother man. The Father and His Christ want to make a dwelling in us through the Holy Spirit.

God also needs man as His helper in order to reveal His love to the world. He wants to show His love to man. He does not want to leave man all alone and without help—man who is called to be saved through redemption. " 'I will not leave you bereft [like orphans].' " (John 14:18, NEB) And so Jesus also says, " 'The man who has received my commands and obeys them—he it is who loves me; and he who loves me will be loved by my Father; and I will love him and disclose myself to him.' " (John 14:21, NEB)

Who can understand the depth of these words? What a great message it is for the deepest depths and inmost being of our heart. Even a lonely person who is unable to find any human friendship may rest assured that he is never alone. And whoever

Every Man Is a Helper 43

does not *intentionally* forsake God will not be forsaken by God, his Friend. What a serious word! We promise at baptism never again to sin intentionally. So we find in God the Friend who helps us to love our brothers and to be a help to them.

If we are helping our fellowmen with the right love, we will not ask anxiously, "What is demanded of me?" or "What must I do in order to be good?" Instead we will ask, "What help is needed here? What will make this other person happy?" Anyone who has lived at the ocean for any stretch of time has experienced something of nature's power in high and low tide. In friendship and in marriage too there is high tide and low tide. And here too, anyone who wants to help has to exercise much patience—he has to wait for the right hour and yet always be ready for the moment when he can help. How easy it is for the person who wants to help to lose his patience, abandon his efforts, and leave the other person in his need because "he just cannot be helped"! How many people think they are useless, that their lives are empty, because they are not helped with the necessary patience! How often we cannot help a person we love! He is as though trapped in mistrust. There is not even a tiny place in his soul for advice, comfort, or friendship to flood into him. Endless patience is needed in such a situation so that the love shown by that very patience can still win through and conquer the mistrust and lift the person (who is in fact emotionally sick) right out of his loneliness and isolation.

6. THE FIRST SIN OF ALL

The report of the creation says that it was the Serpent first of all who treated God and God's Word as if he were their equal. It cannot be overlooked that the Seducer tried to seduce by using the Word of God, just as with Jesus after He had fasted for forty days in the wilderness. The Serpent—an animal, which like other animals had man as ruler—dared to twist the words of God, his Lord, cast doubt on them, and finally accuse God the Lord of lying and malice. Eve listened to all this with curiosity, and this in itself was a betrayal of God. Possibly God's majesty was shattered in Eve's eyes because an animal was able to treat God and God's Word as he did without God intervening.

How could such blasphemy take place in Paradise? For Eve, the image of the Almighty God in Heaven was shattered. Actually, through her colossal downfall she herself shattered the image of the Lord God because she opened her lustful ears to the Serpent's slander. Let us compare this act with what takes place in young persons who are growing up and becoming independent. The separation of man from God, who is the origin of life as well as its end and goal, means separation from true life. But the separation of a child from its earthly father (who, though he is the physical point of origin of the child's life, is not its end and goal) is a development in the direction of man's destiny, not a turning away from God as with Eve. When a youth detaches himself from his father, he is detaching himself at the same time from his childhood. He is a child no longer; he wants to be grown-up himself now and make his own decisions. In Eve too, there was a process of detachment in the course of which her state of childhood, as a child of God, was shattered.

However, it was not only the forbidden fruit that enticed Eve. The Serpent had promised her she would become like God himself and attain a higher level of insight, of awareness, and so be able to know good and evil. Before the maiden's eyes a new spiritual dimension opened up that until then had played no part in her innocent existence as a child of God. A higher state of spiritual existence was alluring to Eve; it excited her curiosity and vanity, her self-love and desire for superhumanity, the possibility of becoming like God. All this is utter separation from God.

The First Sin of All

Adam was with her. Tradition says he slept, that is he remained in a state of unawareness until the woman Eve awakened him to share with him what she had just learned. The woman, though taken from the man and coming into being later than he, was ahead of him in her development; still today, women mature earlier than men.

Adam was awakened by his beloved Eve. The awareness in her spirit aroused him. Possibly he had never seen her like that before, so alluring in her beauty, so promising in her charm, with such strangely disquieting eyes, glittering between yes and no. The shaking thing is that Adam no longer saw God's countenance. He saw his wife's countenance; he made her his goddess, his mistress, and at her command he too ate. In his blind infatuation he forgot God his Father and Creator, and he forgot God's command. With Eve, the "I" interposed itself between self and God and obscured God; so between Adam and God the seductive "thou"—worship of his wife—pushed its way in and obscured God.

The first sin, then, was also the first act of idolatry. It may well have happened in this way: the woman as well as the man sinned against love, that is, against God, and in their infatuation they made idols of each other. Here the basic sin of false love stands opposed to the basic command of love. To transgress against love for God, against love for the "thou," and against the right love for self—this is the first sin of all.

Surely it is very revealing that Satan, the opponent and caricature of God who is true love, embodies false love; that in tempting a human being, he makes use of just this mirror of love. He looks like love and therefore like fulfillment, which is felt as love. Here love is not fulfillment, but its opposite; it is destruction. How many things happen today that go by the name of love and yet are nothing but destruction and soul-murder! True love wants the person of God to shine through the beloved: God remains the value by which love is measured and the final goal of love's striving. But man, in a false love to the beloved, turns away from the highest good and thereby makes it impossible for God to shine through the beloved. In doing so, man loses his center, the criterion of his strivings, as well as the purposeful direction of his powers.

In view of the close connection between love and sex, the offense against love in the first sin has often—understandably—been regarded as a sexual offense. But even in view of this unlikely interpretation, we must hold on very firmly to the fact that, like all sin, this first sin too was a spiritual action and not something born of the flesh. It was the desire to be like God. It was what the Serpent

The First Sin of All

tempted Eve with. This is a deep sickness in the human spirit.

Augustine energetically opposes the idea of shifting the guilt to the flesh when he writes:

> If the flesh is represented to be the cause of all moral defects, this really leaves out of account man's nature as a whole. It is an error to ascribe all the soul's evil to the body. The transitory nature of the body, which weighs down the soul, is *not* the cause of sin but the punishment for it. It was not the perishable flesh that caused the soul to sin; rather the sinful soul has made the flesh perishable. And now many incentives to sin and even sinful desires themselves arise out of this corruption of the flesh. Still we cannot ascribe all vices of an evil life to the flesh. Otherwise we would completely relieve the Devil, who has no flesh, of the burden of this whole matter.
>
> (Augustine, *City of God,* XIV, 3)

7. DIFFERENT AREAS OF THE SENSUOUS

So it was the Serpent who tempted with the words of God. It should not be underestimated that Satan tempted Eve with words of God and that he tempted Jesus with words of God. There is also no doubt that the Antichrist, who is prophesied by Christ, will try to tempt men with words of God. My father, Eberhard Arnold, used to say that sin is the same as separation. We have to think very deeply to understand these words. In the Garden of Eden, sin meant separation from God. We can look at the world today, at men's lives, and see how corrupt this generation is, how impure, and how murderous. Yet we do not straightaway recognize sin as separation. We would perhaps recognize it still less if we were to make friends with all those people who make up a nation or the world. I am quite certain that we would find many very likeable people among them. Why is it then that the world is so corrupt? The answer is: because of separation.

Let us think of man, how he is made: he is spirit, soul, and body. The main thing in man is his heart—not the physical organ but the center of his inner life. The heart decides what spirit a man follows. Man is created as a sensuous being. He experiences everything first of all on the sensuous level. With sensuousness I do not mean only sex, of which the world today is full, but almost everything one experiences. When a young couple have their first child and the child smiles for the first time, they are able to enjoy this only through their senses; without eyes they could not enjoy it. It can be a great gift from God to enjoy something with our senses, but only if it is to the praise and honor of God and in the joy of community with one another. My father explained to me what a wonderful gift godly music is, but never for its own sake. If it becomes independent and worldly, that is to say, if it becomes detached from the experience of the Church and from God and is loved only for its own sake, then it is sin.

This holds good for all spheres of the sensuous. Everything we experience with our senses of hearing, taste, and smell, as well as other senses (quite apart from the sexual) must never be honored separated from God. It can be a joy to smell the scent of a beautiful bouquet of flowers. We can do this to the honor of God or it can become idolatry.

Different Areas of the Sensuous

This is also true the other way round when we go into a slum area and want to hold our noses to keep out the foul smells. There too the sensuous sphere must be under God's rule. If our sense of smell becomes detached from God, we will want to get away as fast as we can. But if we and our sense of smell are under God's leading, the love of God will win the day.

When young people fall in love, a boy with a girl or a girl with a boy, and they find each other's hearts, all that gives them joy at first sight is sensuous—they can look into one another's eyes and hear one another speak; it can be on a deeper level than hearing, tasting, and smelling but still an experience of the senses. The attraction of a boy to a girl belongs very much to the sensuous sphere, and there is in fact nothing wrong in the senses. Whether we sleep, eat, or drink, it is a sensuous experience. When I go out with my wife into the woods in the evening and we experience the wonderful moonlight, it is a sensuous experience, our senses enjoy it.

In a certain way we share the sphere of the senses with the animals. But much more is given to man than to the animal. And God expects more from man than from the animal. Many nice people in the world have joy only in sensuous things. They reject what is evil and what breaks the Ten Commandments: adultery, excess in sexuality, stealing, and so on. But they live without God in a completely sensuous world, even if that world does include love and faithfulness between husband and wife, earning a living for children, and trying to be good parents. From the point of view of God, theirs is a sinful life because it is separated from God. To listen to Bach's *St. Matthew Passion* just to give pleasure to our senses, in spite of the fact that it is very deep music and has the deepest words, would be a sin in the eyes of God because it would be separated from God. *Isolation from God is in itself the sin.*

When we give our hearts to God, everything becomes new. Then if we go out in the evening to experience a forest in beautiful moonlight, we enjoy God the Creator, see God as Friend, and enjoy the beauty of His creation. If we listen to the *St. Matthew Passion* with hearts dedicated to God, the serious words strike our hearts and the singing helps to deepen the experience so that we feel God also through our senses. The experience of joy when a little child is born, when he smiles for the first time and gives his first sign of love—this, we have seen, belongs also to the sensuous sphere. If we are completely dedicated to God, completely His own, we experience God behind that mystery. But without God, parents are in danger of treating their children as idols. To idolize one's children and to protect them from recognizing the evil in pride or any other sin, and

Different Areas of the Sensuous

from feeling remorse, can lead to mental disturbance in the children. There is also a danger that two people idolize each other in marriage, and I want to warn every couple against doing this. If we bear fruit on the tree of idolatry, the harvest will be a bitter one. In order to be healthy in spirit we need to honor and glorify God. If we are no longer able to glorify God or honor father and mother, we are really sick in our soul and spirit.

Here I want to repeat that sin is separation and that even one of the most noble things like singing Handel's *Messiah* can be a sin in the eyes of God when we do not honor God through it. In what is said above, an ungenuine piety is certainly not meant. How seriously Jesus warns us against false piety! In everything the senses experience, the joy in creation should be free of all false piety. That is what my father understood by the idea behind the Youth Movement in Germany: everything should become genuine, childlike, and natural; yet God should be honored above all. And the same should be true of singing. On no account should my words be understood to mean that we should sing nothing but hymns; a natural, childlike joy belongs to the sphere of the senses no matter in what area. Our whole life, with the exception of our religious life, is lived through what we experience by means of the senses. Nor is there anything wrong in this; it only needs to come under God's sovereignty, it must be ruled by the Spirit. All the wonderful things we experience in God's creation are taken in through our senses: we *see* a beautiful landscape, we *see* our brother, we *hear* his voice and *feel* his handshake, we *hear* the birds in the woods, we *see* and *smell* the flowers—and all these things give us enjoyment. With all our senses we see and perceive the human being, the beloved brother or sister whom God has destined for us. It is good that this is so. When sensitivity is lacking in the senses, as for example when a person cannot hear, it is not by any means an advantage! But what is important is that all these things come under God and are ruled by Him. This happens through God's Spirit speaking in *our* spirit and to *our* soul and in *our* heart.

I believe that latent within the human heart are great possibilities of experiencing the most glorious things—we have no inkling of how great. The more we let God rule our senses and the more we give ourselves to God, the greater is the possibility that the heart's deepest longing will be fulfilled. The heart longs only for what is genuine. Deep down, our hearts suffer when we are ungenuine. God does not want to turn us into "pious" people; He wants to make us God-fearing children. The experience of freedom is included in all this. Only in God is freedom. The Youth Movement in Germany with

Different Areas of the Sensuous

its truthfulness and genuineness pointed the way to childlike freedom.

In this book we speak especially about marriage, and in marriage the sensuous sphere plays a very great role. Already in the morning when a couple awake and look into one another's eyes and enjoy their love to one another, it is a blessing only if this love is completely dedicated to God and His Jesus. If it is isolated from God, it belongs to the world of sin. This is very specially true for the intimacy of the marriage relationship. The veil of intimacy between a young man and a virgin must not be lifted without special sanction from God. Both must feel that God led them together; both, in front of the whole Church, must promise their loyalty to one another until death; but still that loyalty to Christ and His Church is even higher than their loyalty to one another.

So we have to come to the following conclusion: the Devil brings separation; God is unity. In God the sensuous world is not despised; He created it. It is only when it becomes an end in itself, when it is isolated and separated, that the sensuous life becomes sinful. God has joy when a young couple experiences full uniting: first in spirit, then from heart to heart and soul to soul, and then one body melting into another. God has joy if this veil is lifted in reverence before Him, in relationship with

Him, and in the unity given by Him; and this we wish our young couples.

Jesus says in His last prayer before the crucifixion: "May they all be one: as thou, Father, art in me, and I in thee, so also may they be in us, that the world may believe that thou didst send me." (John 17:21, NEB) This is my greatest wish for all married couples in the Church, that they give witness to Jesus alone. I think we are not yet able to conceive or to feel with our senses what it means to be just as united with one another as Jesus is with the Father. To God's glory we have to say that we have experienced hours of deep unity in the Church, but I think the glory and beauty of this unity would completely overwhelm us if we could recognize it in its fullness!

In the Beatitudes in the Sermon on the Mount, our Lord and Savior Jesus Christ gives purity a unique position: the pure in heart shall see God. The very thing that is the ultimate goal for all creatures will be revealed to the pure in heart in a special way: to behold God, to have eternal, indestructible community with God.

At first some may think the nature of purity is immediately obvious: after all, every man's conscience tells him what is an offense against purity. But this is a misconception. There are completely

Different Areas of the Sensuous

false and contradictory points of view about the question of purity. A man's conscience does not necessarily tell him that it is sinful to eat a great deal of good food, even though gluttony is expressly mentioned among the great sins in the New Testament. The Apostle Paul says very clearly in his Letter to the Galatians:

> Anyone can see the kind of behaviour that belongs to the lower nature: fornication, impurity, and indecency; idolatry and sorcery; quarrels, a contentious temper, envy, fits of rage, selfish ambitions, dissensions, party intrigues, and jealousies; drinking bouts, orgies, and the like. I warn you, as I warned you before, that those who behave in such ways will never inherit the kingdom of God.
>
> But the harvest of the Spirit is love, joy, peace, patience, kindness, goodness, fidelity, gentleness, and self-control. There is no law dealing with such things as these. And those who belong to Christ Jesus have crucified the lower nature with its passions and desires. (Gal. 5:19–24, NEB)

If we consider the spheres of eating, drinking, sleeping, or any pleasure of the flesh, we soon see that a lack of depth is characteristic of this kind of experience. Anything that belongs to this sphere is superficial, and people who have these experiences in the foreground of their lives are considered superficial. Eating and drinking become sinful when the sensuous sphere rules man and his thoughts and feelings. Then there is no room for God. We have to make it clear to ourselves that God has given the human heart an unbelievable capacity for deep inner experiences. If we let eating and drinking fill all the capacity of our heart, then we are sinning.

A different matter entirely is the glass of water that revives a man dying of thirst, the morsel that puts strength into a starving man, and the bed that receives a man who is dead tired. Because this need is deep, the experience of being released from the need is also deep. Sickness or intense physical pain for example belong to the sphere of deeply felt physical experience, just as the deliverance from it does. When a man dying of thirst craves for a drink of water, it has nothing to do with greed or lust as such, nor with the harmless, good-natured animal-likeness. It awakens our compassion to meet a man dying of thirst—we revive him with a glass of water. But unrestrained joy in good food is animal-like, though it is often very good-natured and for that reason seems to the superficial eye not a sin in such a terribly deep sense.

In contrast to the above areas of bodily experience, the sensual sphere in the narrower sense of sex is *really* and *essentially* deep. Everything that takes place here involves the soul far beyond the limits of the body. The physical experiences meant here are

Different Areas of the Sensuous

totally different from the other experiences of the senses mentioned earlier. The attraction exerted by the other appetites also cannot be compared with the psychological attraction of sex. The deep-going sensuality of sex has certain essential elements that penetrate to the very roots of man's physical being and directly into his soul. They have a depth and an earnestness that lift them far beyond the territory of any other bodily experience. Sensuousness in the area of sex is closely related to the deeper experiences of mind and spirit.

If a man falls so low that he surrenders himself completely to the lusts of impurity, he is defiled thereby in quite a different way than by gluttony. Impurity wounds man in his innermost heart and being. It is sin in quite a different, new way; it attacks the soul. There is something in its nature that harms the soul at its core. A man who lives in impurity corrupts his whole soul. In impurity man gives himself up to impure spirits in quite a unique way.

The sensual sphere in its sexual aspect has a central place in man because first of all body and soul and spirit meet here as they do in no other area of experience. The sexual life affects the spirit, heart, and soul of man in a very deep sense. Secondly, the sexual life has an intimacy all its own, which the individual instinctively hides from others. Sex is *his* secret, something that he feels touches on his inmost being. Every disclosure in this sphere opens up something intimate and personal and lets another person into his secret. Therefore the area of sex is also essentially the area of shame. We are ashamed to unveil this secret before others.

How dreadful is a time and age in which shamelessness has taken over, in which man so despises himself and his human worth that all sense of shame is lost. The modesty or immodesty of a person depends, in the first place, on the attitude of that person toward purity. For the pure man this sphere is each individual's own "secret." When the secret of the pure man is uncovered, it takes place in a unique way as a complete surrender of self in wedlock to the one unique person.

8. THE SACREDNESS OF THE MARRIAGE ACT

Sex is intrinsically intimate and mysterious and should remain so. This brings it into a particularly close connection with love, the deepest and most spiritual of all experiences. This unity between love and sex in marriage cannot possibly be explained exclusively by the purpose of propagation. It would be a serious error to believe that when two people meant by God for each other become one flesh, it is solely for the purpose of procreation. It is simply not true that marriage is purposeful only in this limited sense. Marriage is meant to picture the unity and faithfulness between God and His people.

Faithfulness in marriage is of crucial importance for the inner life of each partner. There is a deep connection between married love in its spiritual and emotional aspects on the one hand and sexual union on the other. When it is given in marriage for two to become one flesh, this physical uniting has a very deep connection with God. Should this relationship become separated from God, it becomes a sinful thing even within marriage. Having a marriage certificate does not give us the freedom to live for the body and its appetites, separated from God.

We should realize that God loves marriage and wedded love, and it is not at all difficult for two childlike hearts to seek and find this union in God. But woe to us if we seek this union separate from God! When each partner gives himself in complete surrender to the other in marriage, an unparalleled uniting takes place because of the unique intimacy and mystery connected with the sexual sphere. This uniting therefore is the organic expression of married love, whose very goal is the mutual giving of self. Each partner knows the secret of the other, and it is God's will that only this one man and this one woman should have such a relationship and not pass it on to someone else.

The present time, so filled with impure spirits, impure literature, impure films and television performances, shows a monstrous overestimation of the role of sex. Yet the sexual relationship is by no means the most important part of the marriage relationship. The representations of sex on bookstalls and newsstands in Europe and America today exaggerate its significance in a thoroughly unhealthy way. Love between man and woman is seen only in an animal sense, as a sexual impulse. The true significance of

The Sacredness of the Marriage Act

love and of this highest of all spiritual acts is utterly missed.

We can understand the true nature of love without referring at all to the existence of sex. In fact, this is the *only* way we can understand what is genuine in any act of love. Its source is divine love, the love that wells up from the heart of Jesus. In this heart of Jesus, every thought of sex between man and wife is cleansed and purified right from the beginning. The act of union in marriage not only has the purpose of begetting children; it also has a meaning for the individuals themselves. It is an expression and fulfillment of love and community in marriage, and it participates in a certain sense in the holy significance of marriage. To hold marriage to a purely utilitarian function would be to rebel against God's creation. In the eyes of God, the unity and love between two people is a deep symbol. And the Apostle Paul speaks of marriage, adding, "I take it [the mystery of marriage] to mean Christ and the Church." (Eph. 5:22, RSV) Such are the holy terms in which marriage is presented. For this reason sex needs to be completely subordinated to God. It is a terrible thing when the sexual sphere in marriage is detached from God.

The real nature of sex, in which two people become one flesh, can only be understood in relation to Eternity. This understanding of the mystery of married love can be given only by Christ himself. The moment the sensual or sexual sphere is treated as an end in itself and isolated from God, the soul becomes defiled and sick. Certainly, sex is something distinct from love; yet we can speak of a deep harmony between sex and married love.

The idea that marriage exists only for a utilitarian purpose is a terrible one (although it must be admitted that the Montanists, a revival group in early Christian times, believed in it). It vanishes when we realize that marriage is given mainly so that two people may become one in spirit, soul, and body. It is sinful in any case to speak of human beings in terms of their usefulness. It is sinful to ask what is the use of raising children who are abnormal, or what is the use of caring for old people. The whole train of thought connected with this idea of use or purpose is contrary to the love of Jesus. It is utterly opposed to the Sermon on the Mount and to apostolic early Christianity. Every man who is born is an object of love and worthy of care, and we are often at the receiving end when we take care of the sick and old. Jesus says expressly: "What you have done to the least of my brothers, you have done to me." (Matt. 25:40)

It is equally wrong, however, to regard the physical union in marriage as the means, and wedded love as the end; for wedded love is the necessary basis for

The Sacredness of the Marriage Act

physical union in marriage. It is a much deeper, entirely new relationship, and a significant one. The act of wedded community has the *object* of begetting offspring; but apart from this, it has the *meaning* of a unique uniting in love. It is different with the other senses.

In the act of communion in marriage, the extent to which both partners participate inwardly in the union is a matter of deepest significance. Sensual participation is not what is meant here, but a participation of hearts. In union in marriage, inner participation is necessary; otherwise it becomes something animal. For a human being, eating, digesting, and breathing are basically the same as for an animal. But intercourse in marriage is unthinkable unless the whole human being takes part—spirit, soul, and body.

Finally, we must understand once more that everything in the sphere of the senses is a mystery. To begin with, it is a mystery because it is experienced as a gift from God. We should thank God before and after every meal because He satisfies our hunger and thirst. It is a fact that the life of the senses has a mysterious meaning, not only in marriage but in all of physical life. Beyond this, since marriage is a mysterious event, it cannot be mere chance that God in His love truly sanctifies the creative marriage act and makes it a symbol and a reality; nor can it be mere chance that in this sacred union, in love and arising out of love, a new human being comes into life. A very old prayer used at weddings speaks completely in this spirit: "O Lord our God, Thou hast created man pure and spotless and thereafter didst ordain that in the propagation of the human race a new image of God be created through the holy love of two, through the mystery of marriage."

In order to grasp the meaning of this mystery, we have to take into account the whole depth of what it means for two to unite in love. Only when we have understood the special relationship between the sexual sphere and wedded love can we grasp in its fullness, depth, and sublimity the relationship between the sexual sphere and the origin of a new human being; only then can we do justice to the fact that this is no mere living thing but a *human being* that comes into life. Man stands before this mystery, before its depth and centrality. It is crucial for man to open his heart completely to the depth and intimacy of this uniting. Only then can he honor his partner and, in reverence, truly love.

In marriage, man unveils the secret of a fellow human being in a unique and intimate way. What man is led to in this area is full of mystery: either the union of two human beings takes place to the glory of God, or a man flings himself *and* God away. He surrenders his secret, delivers himself over to base flesh, and desecrates and violates what God

The Sacredness of the Marriage Act

gave to man alone as His image, thereby separating himself in a terrible way from God. Mysterious as this sacred act of becoming one flesh in marriage is, it can become the abyss of sinfulness if it is abused. Again it cannot be expressed strongly enough that this sexual sphere, as the origin of a new man, can be grasped in its depth and centrality and done justice to only when we have grasped this mystery in our hearts: it is no mere living thing, but a *man* who comes into being, a man made in the image of God.

9. WITH OR WITHOUT GOD?

Man was created for God, and if he points faithfully toward God he will have a great task in creation.

I doubt if a man who has a long struggle with impurity can understand the mysterious character, the depth, centrality, and intimacy of the sexual sphere. If we think of the mystery of wedded love, we realize that in marriage man surrenders himself in a unique way. It is a dreadful sin to provoke God through superficiality in this area. (Even for married people, sexual intercourse without God is dreadful.) Fornication and adultery separate man from God; if we separate ourselves from God *within marriage,* we also provoke God. A marriage certificate is no guarantee for purity.

Let us look at the divine tenderness of the sexual sphere. It was created for love. Yet we see in this day and age what terrible sin there is in this whole area! When two people become completely one in spirit, body, and soul *with God* and *in God,* the sexual sphere is of an extremely tender and mysterious nature, uniting in the most intimate and inexpressible way. It glorifies God. Everything depends on whether it takes place with or without God. As soon as sex is isolated and sought for its own sake to satisfy our lust through sexual intercourse, something terrible happens. Then the depth, seriousness, and mystery disappear to make room for mere fascination, excitement, and intoxication. Separated from God, marriage is a terrible falling away from the image of God. Where this sexual sphere is entered in an unlawful form, as nowadays among millions of young people both in Europe and America, the sensual and sexual desire in a man is poisoned. Such a man will never experience the solemn joy that is so moving, the bliss of the chaste, intimate, and mysterious surrender in a marriage given by God; this marriage reflects something of the image of God.

The unique nature of this sphere can take two very different forms: the one is awe-inspiring, mysterious, noble, chaste, and peaceful; it has a redeeming effect on man. The other becomes a forbidden surrender to naked lust, which makes the soul of man sick. Such sin not only gives the sexual sphere a fascination all its own but makes it the domain of evil lust, which then has a diabolical appeal to man.

With or Without God?

We must not underestimate the armies of impure spirits that, under Satan, drive man to evil. We must not play with impurity, for it will put us under the dominion of demons. Then we experience an eerie, sultry atmosphere, which makes a pure man almost unable to breathe. What was a wonderful experience of God, a gift of God, then becomes a terrible, sinister, and life-destroying experience. What in the one is clear as light—awe-inspiring, illuminating, and holy—is in the other sultry, stifling, confusing, and horrible. This is true not only in prostitution but also when a person serves the spirit of impurity on his own body and satisfies himself through impure actions. A man should not believe he can indulge in impurity on his own body without suffering harm from it; it cannot be said strongly enough that he is hurting God in doing so. He is awakening evil spirits and letting them dwell within him. Then a very evil atmosphere comes from such a man. He is opening his heart to devils of whose cruel character he has no inkling.

How very different it is in a God-given marriage! The elements of intimacy, tenderness, mystery, and deep uniting are the true, God-willed qualities of this area. What a deep joy it is for a couple to know that God sees them in this deepest union! He blesses them in a very specific way! It is God who blesses the marriage. The deep bliss both experience springs from a union such as God alone can give. In this unique union each partner gives and reveals himself in the most intimate things, knowing that the union is willed by God. When God rules and speaks in marriage there is no *seduction* in it but something liberating, moving, solemn, and deeply serious.

We cannot be silent about the dangerous character of the sexual sphere. The evil demon comes in all forms—in seducing and alluring forms—in order to kill the pure, God-given relationship. This impure spirit can creep even into the sanctuary of marriage. But there it is a foreign element, and when such a thing happens there will have to be serious repentance: we have to do not only with our own sensuality but with evil spirits. When impurity creeps into marriage, our eyes are no longer focused on love. Impurity has within it something irreverent, degrading, and corroding.

It is the tragedy of fallen man that at least the *danger* of this perversion is always present, the danger of allowing the sexual sphere to become an end in itself and thereby separate from God. *This is a terrible and poisoning sin.* But to the degree that God gains victory over a man's life, to the same degree is that man set free. Full of joy even in pain, he is a true reflection of God's image.

There is a tremendous contrast between sex as the mystery of love and sex as the vehicle of diabolically

With or Without God?

evil lust. The poisonous enchantment of evil lust takes over when sex is isolated from God. I warn everyone who plays with impurity: you will not be able by yourself to drive away the evil spirits you allow to enter. They have gained power over your soul. A very special intervention of Jesus Christ is needed to free you from those evil spirits.

We find the opposite in a God-given marriage. Here there is a deaf ear to all impure and sordid images. These images are incompatible with a pure marriage. We can recognize the true nature of sex only when we can see in it true seriousness, intimacy, mystery, and unity—that is, when it is given to us as the fulfillment of wedded love and we know that it is sanctioned by God.

10. WHAT IS IMPURITY?

Man's purity involves a very definite attitude to the extraordinary sphere of sex. Whether a person is pure or impure depends most of all on his stand in this area of life.

Let us ask first of all, "In what does impurity consist?" It consists in the abuse of sex. When someone flings himself away with no intention of forming an eternal bond, he is prostituting himself. The act that represents a unique giving of oneself and the deepest, most intimate union, becomes a squandering of self when it is not founded on married love and the express will for a lasting community, one that is not subject to caprice. It is a betrayal of self and of others, and of God first and foremost; it spells ruin to the character and opens the heart to impure spirits and demons.

The starkest form of this impurity occurs when a person gives himself to another in the most intimate way merely for the sake of satisfying his sexual desires, when he uses the body of another to gratify himself and pays for it with money without feeling even for a moment a deep albeit fleeting love. Such a person "becomes one with a harlot," as the Apostle Paul warns us so very seriously; or the poor harlot becomes one with the fornicator. The marriage act signifies the consecrated union of two human beings in one flesh. It is meant to be the expression and fulfillment of an enduring and indissoluble bond of love. It represents the supreme surrender to another because it involves the mutual revelation of a secret, a self-revelation of the most intimate kind. To perform this act without being united in the bond of marriage is the most terrible kind of desecration.

Desecration of any sort is sin; for example, if I desecrate anything that belongs to God, or if I abuse a human being by treating him as a thing instead of a human being, I violate his dignity as an image of God. I do not have enough reverence for him. So too, it is sinful desecration of another human being to seduce him or her to become one flesh through sexual intercourse, without any thought of one's own responsibility for the other's soul or for his love and faithfulness. It is an even more terrible sin to seduce a person of the same sex. It is godless and perverse to ruin the lives of boys. The early Church gives a particularly serious warning against this. Impurity is always present when the sexual sphere is used in any way that is forbidden. To abuse a human being

What Is Impurity?

for the satisfaction of one's own desire, ignoring spirit and soul, is a terrible crime against the other's spirit, soul, and body *and* against one's own.

The same horrible destruction of a soul made in God's image takes place when someone gratifies his sexual impulses on his own body. It is always a desecration to employ something destined for a sublime end in a manner contrary to its high destiny. In the same way as royalty would be debased by being enslaved, so man debases his noble destiny as an image of God when he abuses his own body sexually.

This brings us back to the essence of impurity, the separation of sensuality and sex from God and from the human spirit and heart. The consequences to the human heart are absolutely appalling. Sex for its own sake has two aspects: enticing, sensual attraction with its poisonous sweetness, and diabolic, evil lust. Both are like the bites of a snake: their poison corrodes and destroys souls. These aspects of sex are not understood nowadays, least of all by psychologists.

Finally, the abuse of sex also defiles and besmirches a person in a particular way when he misunderstands the nature of sex and abandons himself to it unthinkingly, treating it merely as a source of pleasure. This is true of the dull, bestial impurity that characterizes the fleshly man. He has a false idea of sex and treats it like the pleasure of eating. He seeks the physical pleasure of sex solely for the pleasure in it and has no understanding of its special nature. Such a person sinks below the level of an animal. A very definite kind of defilement takes place (quite apart from the debasement and desecration), a bondage to the flesh entirely different from a surrender to the pleasure of eating for example. Such a person may believe that sexual pleasure differs only in degree from other kinds of pleasure, but the carnal degrading of the spirit through surrender to naked lust differs from gluttony in kind, not merely in degree. The person concerned may put the pleasure of sex in the same category as that of eating, but abandonment to the flesh has a destructive effect on the spirit incomparably more far-reaching and different in kind. To understand this we need to recognize the fundamental tendency of the sexual sphere, when brought into full play, to engulf the spiritual.

The mindless, bestial surrender to sexual pleasure is a blatant example of the spirit of a person being submerged in the physical. Such a person, however, is not like the sinner who gives himself to the attraction of sex or even to demonic, evil lust. He is not submerged in the vital stream of his being but in lifeless material existence—it matters little whether the sin is against his own body or against another's, but in the second case, as well as ruining his own soul he ruins the soul of another person made in

God's image. Of course, such a carnally impure person also differs from the glutton in that he is guilty of fearful desecration and degradation.

There is also an impure sensuality in people who seek and find a certain sensual gratification in their love of sensation, their love of professional sports for example, and in those who crave for power and thereby enslave their fellowmen. Such people, if they have not sinned in the sexual area, often consider themselves better than those who have. They may speak with aversion of sex in marriage. They lack the freedom of the truly pure man. The clear light, the freedom of the light, the freedom of the pure, is not theirs.

11. THE INSENSUOUS PERSON

Insensibility, the lack of response in the senses, is not purity. This cannot be emphasized enough. Many people think that complete lack of sexual feeling (which may be inborn) is complete purity. But the absence of sensitivity is not even necessarily a fertile ground for purity. When we speak of sensual or sensuous people, we are often thinking of those with strongly developed instincts. We mean people who are vitally alive in contrast to certain ethereal natures who make a gentle or spiritual impression and in contrast to those who are weary or lifeless. How far inherited instincts are present or lacking shows itself in different spheres, among them the sexual, but it is no proof of purity or impurity. The spiritually-minded man will seek to control his instincts by his will. His natural disposition does not tell us how far he achieves mastery over them; it does not prove anything.

People who see lust in the same way as they see

gluttony do not understand the intimacy of the sexual sphere, nor do they recognize the seductive charm of demonic evil lust. They have powerful instincts but lack an understanding for the special nature of the sexual sphere. We should not call them sensuous. They should rather be called fleshly. A fleshly temperament gives a man nothing of the sensitiveness and intensity that goes hand in hand with genuine sensuousness. It even makes him coarse.

The man who lacks sensibility to sex is in actual fact an incomplete man. A door to deep experiences is closed to him. He lacks something that is indispensable to making a complete man of him, not only in his natural disposition—he lacks something that gives color to his whole nature. Sensibility to sex permeates human nature far beyond the sexual sphere. The nature of man is formed through his sensibilities. What is a lack in the insensuous man is fullness in the sensuous man. The *pure* man is the only *complete* man. In him is life in its fullness.

Above all we must bear in mind—and this is something quite decisive—that both sensibility and insensibility are merely natural dispositions, like a lively or a passive temperament. Purity, on the contrary, is never a matter of disposition in the sense of being inborn. The distinction between virtue and natural disposition is largely determined by the part played by the person himself. When we speak of natural disposition we mean a man's constitutional makeup which, like his physical characteristics, he cannot influence. From the beginning of their years of maturity, there clings to some people a chastity for which they have not had to struggle. Similarly there are people with great delicacy of feeling. To some it is given at birth; others have to strive for it. But there is a divine quality of purity that must be *given by God*. When in the Beatitudes Jesus blesses the pure and meek, He speaks of a purity and meekness that are not inborn. They are always associated with divine love and are always gifts from God.

Genuine meekness always involves the basic attitude of a person. It is always accompanied by a love to one's neighbor and a feeling for his personality and his need. It bears the weaknesses of others. It includes also the will to be meek and a delicate understanding for what is ugly in lovelessness, strife, malicious anger, and cruel force. Genuine meekness is an inner gift arising from complete surrender to God. Everything depends on our finding this full surrender to God. Purity of heart depends on it, the quality of true meekness depends on it—all the qualities mentioned in the Beatitudes depend on it.

The humble man can experience the infinite greatness and goodness and majesty of God. The proud man never can. The humble man can experience God so powerfully that his heart shouts with joy, his innermost being glows. To the proud man the experience of God remains closed. The humble man yields himself wholly to God and wants to live, not in his own strength, but only through God and for His glory. So the truthful man is aware of the inner beauty of truthfulness and the loathsomeness of deceit, lies, trickery, and inner untruth. He abhors the world of lies and affirms the world of truth.

We have seen that virtue is not a matter of natural disposition. We must also guard against thinking of it in connection with achievement. It is connected with man's relationship to Jesus. A man gripped by Jesus has an extraordinary, light-filled quality. The special beauty of virtue lies in its nature as a gift from God. The more a man is born of the Spirit, the stronger will virtue become and the nearer will he be to his true character as a man. Only Jesus gives a man true character.

In the spiritual person, any virtue (even if it has existed without a struggle from his early youth) is supported at every moment by his basic attitude. In other words the virtue exists only so long as the person is concerned to uphold it. To every virtue clings something of its Creator. This, however, is not yet rebirth. A person in whom certain virtues are inborn may at times not be particularly gentle or good, even though these qualities are inborn in him. But if he does not uphold them and gives himself up to dissipation, the beauty of his inner life breaks down. If he turns to evil, he falls even if he has inherited the most wonderful gifts; for instead of seeking God he is seeking only himself, and the man who seeks only himself detaches himself from God. All his virtues turn into arrogant, covetous vice. Then all his gifts have nothing in common with divine virtues. Any virtue can be struggled for later in life, but it can be received only *as a grace* and gift from God. If an angry, violent man suddenly becomes gentle, it is a sign that he has been born again of God. Such a transformation can only be a victory of God, which has perhaps been preceded by a long and wearisome struggle.

These distinctions between virtue and natural disposition help us to understand the difference between purity and sexual insensibility, which turn out to be quite different from each other. Insensibility may be just a matter of natural disposition, but a man with true purity has received it from God in rebirth. He takes a clear attitude to the world of impurity. He radiates purity.

The so-called inborn insensibility (which must never be confused with rebirth) is simply a lack of appreciation of both the positive and negative aspects of the sensual sphere. For instance, a totally unmusical person does not appreciate the world of musical tones. To his ear the most wonderful melody is just as much a jumble of sound as the worst kind of music. Being insensible in general has nothing to do with being able to discern worth or worthlessness. True discernment has to be given by the grace of God in rebirth. The human voice is a gift of the Creator just as much as a wonderful moonlit night is. But like all pleasures of the senses, singing takes on its true meaning for the first time when it is experienced under God.

In complete contrast to sexual insensibility, the purity given through rebirth brings with it a discernment of good and evil in the sensual sphere and at the same time the right response. This in itself is enough to make us look at the profound difference between purity and insensibility as God reveals it. Whether a thing is an abomination or whether it is wonderful because it comes from God cannot be solved by considering the difference between sensitiveness and insensitiveness.

Insensibility and purity are in no way identical; this we have seen. Insensibility is not an especially fertile ground for purity—it does not make it easier. Its relationship to purity is like that of sluggishness to gentleness, not like that of delicacy of feeling to gentleness. What natural disposition does make the

The Insensuous Person

virtue of purity easier? Surely the opposite of the fleshly nature: namely, a general tenderness of the passions, a delicacy of feeling, a sensitiveness—a temperament that reflects spirit rather than matter. It is not the absence of sensitiveness but the presence of tender feeling (in contrast to strong passions) that is decisive for the disposition in which purity can thrive.

Sensuousness as we mean it goes together with delicacy of feeling, which keeps its character as a favorable ground for purity and modesty. In fact sensuousness enhances it. A man whose senses are awake to the intrinsic qualities of the sexual sphere is thereby naturally equipped to discern both the good and the evil that arise in this area. He has a discernment that the insensuous man must acquire from without, laboriously as it were, if he wants the virtue of purity. A man with this sensuous disposition has the delicate, refined nature that in no situation lets go and becomes loud and boisterous. He has an instinctive shyness, which shrinks from exposing its secrets to a glaring light. And he has an instinctive tendency to draw back from the dark, unknown element that lies hidden in the sexual sphere.

No one, then, is pure simply because he is insensitive. The man who is insensitive to sex can even be impure. Being insensitive to sex, the alternatives of *pure* or *impure* in the deepest sense do not apply to him. If a man wants to be pure, purity must be deeply grounded in his innermost heart as a grace. Since insensitiveness is actually a deficiency, it is in itself worthless even though it is not morally wrong. It would not be right to regard insensitiveness to sex as desirable, let alone as the apex of purity.

12. THE PURE IN HEART

The pure man feels the seriousness and intimacy of the sexual sphere deeply within his heart. He senses the mystery of it. He knows of the wonderful destiny of the sexual sphere and how terrible it is and how frightfully murderous for man's soul when the sexual sphere is abused, when it is separated from God and used for its own ends.

A pure man senses how the abuse of sex opens doors to evil spirits who are awakened through impure actions and from whom a man cannot free himself on his own. That is why the pure man fears anything that defiles the soul and separates it from God; he senses the poison in the sexual area when sex becomes an end in itself. In this connection it should be clearly said that it is a terrible sin for any girl or woman to use her physical attractions to tempt men, which is what vanity does. It leads others into sin. It has no room in a life of brotherhood.

This question of sex becoming an end in itself is a decisive question also in marriage. When the true relationship to God and the Church is missing, the sexual area becomes sinful. It is an illusion to think that all struggles in this area come to an end as soon as one is married. On the contrary, they only begin then. I cannot say it sharply enough that as an end in itself the sexual sphere poisons the heart of man; he opens his heart to a serpent whose bite is deadly.

The pure man lives in reverence for the mystery that lies in the sexual area. He in no way despises sex as such. He is free from fear, free from any prudish disgust with regard to sex and the act of wedded love. But he keeps at a respectful distance from it, especially before marriage, until he is called by God to enter its territory. When a young husband and wife are called by God to go into this area, they will have the attitude Moses had when he came upon the burning bush: here is holy ground, take your shoes off. The body of a Christian should be kept completely chaste before marriage.

In finding the right partner, the decisive factor is the unity of heart and soul in the Holy Spirit. The will of Jesus guides the life of every dedicated Christian; He brings together two people who are meant for each other. With absolute trust we can fall into His arms in regard to all questions of life; He will lead us clearly. When He gives this special unity between two people, He gives joy in all aspects of marriage: first the unity of Spirit and faith, second the emotional love from heart to heart, which is especially between one boy and one girl, and third the uniting of one man and one woman to become one flesh. When there are special problems such as differences in character and individual weaknesses, Jesus has the answer and gives healing.

The pure man knows that the sexual sphere *belongs in a special way to God*. Hardly anything in human life—except perhaps deep Church experiences like baptism and the Lord's Supper—shows man's complete dependence on God as does a God-given marriage, in which a man wants to give and accept the expression of love in the sexual sphere. Only with God's express permission may he make use of it. Nothing reveals more plainly the presence of a mystery than this need of a special sanction from God to enter the sexual domain.

All that we have or may one day have belongs to God alone. And we have to keep to this as something holy. Man should be God's steward in his use of all earthly goods; he is not his own master. This is especially true for our Brotherhood. We on the Hutterian Bruderhof say that all our money, all our strength is given to God. In comparison with this and with the area of eating and drinking or intellectual activity, the area of sex belongs in a unique way to God. There is no area where God alone rules in such an intimate and profound way as in the sexual sphere when it is experienced in the unity of two people. The marriage relationship between husband and wife is something quite special. The meeting of two people in this sphere is reserved in a special way to God. God has great joy in the uniting of husband and wife, and to Him it is quite natural if it takes place frequently. Like all spheres of life, this intimate sphere has to be guided by the Holy Spirit. Sexual uniting is meant not only for propagation, but there is a special holiness about it because little souls may be called out of Eternity onto this earth. Man ought to feel an inner awe of this sphere, an awe that other areas do not demand. To the truly pure man this sphere becomes a prayer to God.

The pure man loves chastity. In America and Europe the shamelessness of our time is a sign of the impurity and the remoteness from God in people's lives today. Everything reeks of impurity: advertisements, literature, dress, television, music—they all serve evil and impure demons. The pure man has a deep aversion to any contact with the sexual sphere without the presence of God. He fears such contact. He knows that, when this area is divorced from God and becomes an end in itself, it is an abomination in the eyes of God and a terrible sin, which corrupts his heart through and through.

Eating and drinking also belong to the sensual sphere. It is serious to sin in this area but it does not

The Pure in Heart

have such deeply wounding consequences as sinning in the sexual area. The Apostle Paul warns us of these things seriously (Gal. 5:19–24), and I do not want to fail to tell you the truth in all areas. I believe that we should have our meals only in relationship to God and in thanksgiving, even if we do not make an outward show of it. We should implant this deeply in the hearts of our children.

Concerning fasting, I believe it does no harm to fast sometimes. It frees a person from the danger of the sensual sphere becoming an end in itself. I do not want to put pressure on anyone, but I believe that within certain limits it leads to God. In the New Testament, fasting is not so strongly emphasized, even though Jesus himself fasted for forty days (and this happened after the Holy Spirit had descended upon Him like a dove). I only want to say that it does not harm anyone but could actually give healing to a soul to fast once in a while.

Under God the pure man has no aversion to the sensual and sexual sphere, which is God's domain; he lives constantly in an attitude of reverence for his Creator and for this sphere. This reverence is a basic element of purity and belongs to a Christian attitude. For this reason we have to be very watchful that no irreverence of any kind is tolerated in our children.

The pure man guards his secret and will never lift its veil irreverently. He does not simply conceal his secret from others while he revels in it himself, making himself important. That is the attitude of the prude. It is a sign of our sick age that a man, separated from God, satisfies his sexual lusts on his own body. But that should not be: he has no idea how terribly evil such actions are. The pure man, if he is unmarried, stays right away from this whole area and does not attempt to unveil it. He radiates simple clarity. He leaves it in God's hands in open humility.

In a special sense the pure man walks with God. He never departs from God's presence. He does not hide from God, like Adam and Eve after the fall. His spirit dwells in unclouded light; it is neither corroded by the intoxication of sex nor infected by the sultry atmosphere that clings to the world of evil lust. The pure man senses something alarming when he feels surrounded by the intoxicating poison of impurity and the heavy atmosphere of evil lust, as it is exhibited so shamelessly on many college campuses. Our age, the twentieth century, is full of this evil, sultry impurity.

In the soul of a pure man there is no twilight; he is not surrounded by an atmosphere heavy with poisonous perfume in which it is impossible to breathe freely. The spirit of such a person will not be grieved or clouded before God. He is gifted with a special richness of spirit. The soul that comes from God's hand as His image and is redeemed by Christ has a

The Pure in Heart

characteristic beauty, an undimmed radiance that shines out toward us. In the pure person the light that streams from God can expand and shine forth unclouded. His soul shines before God because it reflects His splendor. A wonderful peace emanates from the pure heart. It is not only a subjective peace, not only a personal peace of heart (which in itself is a wonderful thing); he longs for, seeks, and reflects in his heart the peace and reconciliation of Jesus Christ for all men. But only the man whose heart is filled with *love* is really pure in this sense. The cold and arrogant will never have this brightness of soul.

Further, a pure man is always humble and truthful. He realizes he is a sinner like everyone else, capable of losing himself in the flesh at any moment were he not prevented by God's grace. He is not afraid to recognize and name the dangers that surround him. He does not forget that "the Devil prowls around like a roaring lion, seeking someone to devour." (1 Pet. 5:8) He knows he is made of flesh and blood and is not immune to their weaknesses. In his humility he realizes very clearly that he is capable of falling like anyone else. He is free of the false modesty of the prude. He admits both to himself and others that these dangers exist even if he has never been tempted by impurity. He has a straightforward, childlike attitude. Simplicity, truthfulness, and humility are as much a part of purity as reverence.

Without reverence, the life of the soul is not healthy. Without reverence, we can neither find true marriage nor bring up children. To have reverence and to honor father and mother is most important even for the smallest child. We must be quite clear about that. All that is evil, all that is hostile to God, thrives on the soil of irreverence. The Brotherhood has the task of being alert and tolerating no irreverence among children or adults. We must protect reverence like an eternal flame, for if that is extinguished, everything is lost. Purity, humility, faith, love, hope—all are lost when reverence is extinguished.

Every virtue has a value that needs a response. With every man born of the Spirit, we find a joy in every virtue, a moved response to what comes from God, and an understanding of the good in virtue and the evil in vice. He knows the value of purity. Whenever he meets a pure man, he is aware of that man's purity as something good, its fragrance delights him, and its beauty is appreciated by him. Whenever he meets an impure man, he is aware of his impurity as something evil, and the sight of that man's disease-ridden soul gives him a painful stab in the heart. There can be no looking at his own purity. As with every other virtue, a reflex glance at his own worth is

The Pure in Heart

enough to endanger humility, the foundation of all virtue.

As soon as we think we are pure, compassionate, or kind, we lose humility and all other virtues. Our innermost being will turn cold as ice. It is never good to observe oneself to find out how good or how bad one is. The humble man recognizes the inward beauty of humility; he knows its value and recognizes it in others. It is the same with the pure man. Yet the pure man not only recognizes the virtue of purity but also affirms it and honors it as a gift from God. He rejoices in every pure creature he meets. This exuberant response to purity characterizes the pure man. He lives, so to speak, at the source of God's purity; it sets his heart on fire; he loves it.

Just as much as the pure man loves purity, he hates and abhors impurity. When the upright, pure man stands *in humility before God,* he will really be a help to his brothers. He hates and loathes impurity, but his hatred and loathing will never be turned against a man who struggles and fights for purity. On the contrary, the humility and love in him will draw him to that person, who is already tormented enough by impure spirits. There is no doubt that with an evil deed we open our hearts to evil spirits and give them a foothold through which they can attack our inner lives. Whoever profanes his own body through impurity ruins his own inner life and brings harm to everyone around him. Out of love this cannot be said sharply enough. But this does not mean that the Brotherhood looks upon such a person in a cold and judging way; rather, the Brotherhood loves him and out of love has to tell him what a terrible thing he is doing and how very necessary it is for him to change his heart completely through repentance, conversion, and faith.

What is said above shows the great responsibility of the Brotherhood for seeing that a pure atmosphere rules on every Hutterian Bruderhof. This fight goes hand in hand with the necessity to make room in our hearts for purity. But there is no true purity of heart without a feeling for justice. Not without reason does Jesus say in the Beatitudes: "Blessed are those who hunger and thirst for justice." Purity is related not only to the sexual area: a man defiles his heart if he knows his neighbor is hungry and yet goes to bed without giving him food, simply leaving him to his fate.

A wonderful splendor clings to everything that stands in an unbroken relationship to God; it should actually be experienced as a gift by each baptized member of the Church. The pure man always looks to Christ and has the glory of His light before his eyes. It is Christ toward whom his whole being is turned—Christ who alone is pure. This is purity: surrender to the countenance of God in Heaven before whose splendor the angels sing their songs of praise. It is pleasing to God when two people become completely one in spirit, soul, and body. God rejoices in this unity.

No one should be shaken in his faith if he does not always have Christ so clearly before his eyes. Every Christian experiences such times. We should think of Jesus himself and of His God-forsakenness.[1] Here we want to point to what we should strive for with our whole hearts: complete surrender to this radiance of purity that streams from Jesus. In a pure marriage, both partners surrender to this radiance. Now we can see why the pure man lives in God's presence in a special way, and why God hides His countenance from the impure man even though He loves him and seeks him and wants to cleanse him. God's countenance radiates over the Church that longs for purity and fights for purity.

All things that come from God have this special radiance. The closer they are to His holiness the more this is true. The truly pure man born of the Spirit perceives the splendor of all that is good. But not only this: in a very special way he perceives the radiant splendor of God and surrenders to it. I know from personal experience that every child can feel this closeness to the Father in Heaven. Even very

---

[1] 'My God, my God, why hast thou forsaken me?' (Matt. 27: 46, NEB)

young children can honor the purity and holiness of God in their hearts. It is the task of parents to lead them to this experience.

It is of vital importance for the pure man to reject all the evil that clings to sexual impurity. His attitude to the befogging fascination of demonic evil lust or the coarse pleasures of the flesh can only be one of complete rejection. He reacts instinctively against all this because he knows that as soon as he yields to evil he will be banished from God's countenance. Whether he is susceptible to its seductive language or not, the pure man is aware of the evil that clings to the sexual sphere as an end in itself.

The pure man will have a very positive approach to people from whom true purity streams in the God-ordained expression of unity in wedded love. One might think that purity consists merely in the right attitude in the sexual sphere, in which lies both good and evil; but that would be wrong. When sex fulfills its divinely ordained function, it is mysteriously tender, moving, and peaceful; it creates a unique bond. Then it goes together with other virtues, like depth of soul, tenderness, and self-giving love. Purity certainly demands that the man who enters the sexual sphere surrenders himself only to these values set by God.

13. THE SENSUOUS SPHERE IN MARRIAGE

How does the pure man act when he lifts the veil of the sensuous sphere in marriage and comes to the act of sexual unity with his bride, who is now in God's eyes his wife? The sensuous sphere has a special danger for the spirit of a person. The relationship of husband and wife in the sexual sphere, the physical uniting, is the central act of the body. This moment full of life means a complete fulfillment and awakening for the body—in a certain way, the only moment in which the body comes to its full expression. At this moment, the life of the body returns in a certain way to its roots. The sexual sphere represents the greatest power in the living body, not in the sense of a need, like illness or the need for nourishment, but in the sense of bringing fulfillment to a structure within the human being.

The peak of the uniting of two bodies is called orgasm. This is a powerful and shaking experience and can have a forceful effect on the spirit; it can even have a dangerously forceful effect. In this act there is a danger of the spirit being swallowed up by the physical life, and this in two ways. First, because of the deeply connected unity between body, soul, and spirit, this act of physical uniting is, apart from death, the deepest physical experience. The relationship between body, soul, and spirit is never so deeply touched through the body as in these two experiences: in the uniting of two bodies, and in death.

Is the spirit, in a certain way, independent from the physical being? At least with every Christian it should be a fact that the spirit rules and not the body. Though the spirit is deeply embedded in the physical body, it should be far above, or over, the body and the sensuous sphere. In the act of physical uniting in marriage there is a danger of destroying that rulership of the spirit. Certainly this is only a tendency—it never really happens. The sovereignty of the immortal soul in contrast to the physical life is undamageable in a Christian and a spiritual person. It is only possible to be morally swallowed up when the spirit does not go into the same depths of the experience as the body, when it does not bring the right balance into the experience and keep the rulership over the body. All this shows how dangerous the misuse of the sensuous sphere in the sexual area can become. It is an enormous danger for the man who has fallen into sexual sin, which can be

The Sensuous Sphere in Marriage

forgiven only through a new attitude of the spirit.

There is a second danger of the spirit of a person being swallowed up in orgasm. It is a remarkable experience to give oneself completely—which is what happens in different situations in the emotional life. Let us look first at the way we can lose ourselves in another situation. Someone is suddenly gripped by a panic and rushes off without thinking, terrified, and people say, "He has lost his senses!" In fact, this experience has also the character of a swallowing-up. That person is not able to have full control over himself—he is, so to speak, swept away. Even the normal feeling of being an independent personality is lost for a moment. The person does not want even his own personality anymore. This happens especially if the veil of sexuality is lifted without the sanction of God.

Every passion is dangerous to our inner life—it may be a craze for professional sports or anything else, such as having a delight in sensational news. Every such passion is dangerous for the inner life, and if we *voluntarily* throw ourselves into the arms of such a passion, we will be swallowed up.

This is different with a marriage sanctioned by God. We can even be "swallowed up by" or completely submerged in something very divine. We can be really gripped or submerged in such a way that our hearts are deeply moved and shaken by the goodness of God or by the deepest feeling of remorse. When the experience of the goodness of God or of overwhelming remorse is linked with compassion, then it is a truly deep, spiritual, and religious experience. This fact of being gripped in our innermost person, shaken to the roots of our being, belongs to every true and deep religious experience. In its highest forms, it happens to those people who have a special calling in life and therefore also have special experiences of God. Such experiences do not have the damaging effect of making us love ourselves but lead us all the more deeply and fully into belonging to God, who becomes more and more a present reality.

In spite of the similarity of both experiences, the one completely destroys the inner personality. If we lift the veil of marriage without God, even within marriage, we give ourselves to very powerful physical experiences which are, as I said before, only to be compared with death itself. At such moments we do not belong to ourselves. In the opposite case, when we give our lives completely to God or make a covenant with God in marriage, we belong more and more to God. God is present, also in the intimate sphere of marriage.

When God gives permission (which we really have to experience in our hearts) then the marriage relationship is a great gift from God. It is God himself who melts spirit, soul, and body of two

The Sensuous Sphere in Marriage

people together. To be gripped by the power of sexuality in holy marriage is not sinful at all if we stand under God.

The greatest experience a person can have on this earth, married or unmarried, is to be fully gripped and thrown over by God himself, even if it is by the wrath of God, and all the more wonderful if it is by the goodness of God. But if we step into God's territory (to which marriage belongs) in an impertinent way and follow the commands of our senses, then everything is actually dirt; we even lose ourselves completely. The lifting of the veil between bride and bridegroom belongs to God's territory. *How wonderful it is when two young people do that under God!* He is present with His goodness and rejoices in the uniting of these two. Passion becomes a problem when we lose all control over our emotional inner life and the spirit is pushed aside. In spite of the fact that the two experiences seem to be similar, there is in reality no similarity in them. In a marriage given by God, there is God's blessing over the couple and over the sensuous and sexual area. If they are melted together as one spirit, one heart, and one soul, becoming one flesh (as Jesus expresses it), these married couples are in such moments very close to God and belong to God. God is then closer to them than they are to each other.

To allow passion alone to overcome us can lead us to throw ourselves away completely. It can for instance lead to the most horrible sin, suicide. When we allow ourselves to go close to the abyss with our passionate anger, we are in danger of losing God completely. In such a passion it is possible to give ourselves over to the Devil. When someone says, "If I do not get what I want, then I have no alternative but to commit suicide," this is black rebellion against God. It is black sin against God. It is losing God.

Certainly, the evil passion that comes over us has different degrees. It can start in a small way without, as with suicide, the selling of our souls to the Devil. But the closer we come to giving in to the Devil completely, the more serious it is. We feel a great guilt because we know we have fallen from God's order even if we did not go so far as throwing ourselves away completely. In a certain way, when we cut ourselves off from God's order we lose our inner existence. The only possibility of returning from the abyss is through the compassion of God. We ourselves are absolutely helpless. We have thrown something away that we cannot fetch back. Yet God in His compassion can give us something completely new even if we have lost ourselves in an evil way. We cannot be warned enough of the great sin of abusing the God-created gifts of the body for sexual satisfaction. It will become a curse over our lives, opening

The Sensuous Sphere in Marriage

them to demons and devils. It needs very deep healing because it cuts very deep wounds, with poison eating into the wounds.

If we are under the curse of having set foot on God's territory without His blessing and permission, the *only* help is to seek deep remorse and repentance and the healing that can be given only through Jesus Christ, who reveals the great compassion of God. A person who has a deep feeling for God but has a very strong urge or passion in any area can be protected from doing evil: God wants to protect and shield those who are tempted if they only give Him the opportunity.

There is a blemish attached to the sexual sphere since the fall of man in Paradise, when man wanted to be like God and was filled with a poison that brought death to every man. Like the corruption of the body after death, many things in life are visible consequences of the fall of man. The sexual area in the community of marriage is not excluded. There is a deep-seated danger that can lead to isolated passion and passion to brutality. Brutality has nothing to do with the nobleness and aristocracy of God's Spirit; it belongs to a different atmosphere. In the act of wedded community in its finest form, such elements and moments of brutality are impossible. Love rules the whole situation. The evil elements have to be silent, yet they are silent only if they are changed into something noble, so that an evil situation cannot possibly enter the marriage relationship. But often they are only silenced and not objectively changed into something new, which is possible only through a complete change of heart.

Vital functions that are willed by God, such as the sexual act in marriage, can become brutal if they become independent of God. This brutality can come to life with great power. Our spirit withdraws from its animal-likeness. We are shy of talking about such an intimate area; a feeling of shame makes us not want to go into details; we have too much reverence for this whole sphere created by God. This shyness is very important in a true marriage, yet it can change to a certain degree when two people are so much under the light of God and under the blessing of God that they can talk openly about any part of the sexual life that they find perverse or unworthy of man. These things become small before the great gift of true marriage—love is transformed into real deeds. (In the same way, when a nurse serves the sick she does not feel the importance of being a nurse, but love for her neighbor.) It has to be said very clearly that withdrawing from brutality is something quite different from a reverent shyness before the intimacy of marriage. A reverent shyness has a much more noble and spiritual part in the feeling of chastity than simply withdrawing.

The Sensuous Sphere in Marriage

In what way can the spirit transform this sphere of the senses so that there is no hiding from the good Spirit, so that the shining light of the soul before God is not clouded? Only love can do this, love that can transform the sensuous sphere into something from God. And it cannot be just love, just any love. It must be a love that firstly has a special quality, secondly is blessed by God, and thirdly has a meaning for our neighbor, for the Church, for the cause, for the Cross of Jesus. Married love must be this kind of love. It contains the longing for uniting, and in this, love in marriage has its special place—only there can two find the uniting as one flesh with the blessing of God. Here lies the deep difference between married love and love from brother to sister, from friend to friend: married love has God's blessing to seek and to find the complete uniting of heart, soul, and body.

14. MARRIAGE IN THE HOLY SPIRIT

It is love and love alone that can change and transform the character of the sexual sphere in marriage. Each partner has to regard sexual love as holy—it is not enough for it merely to exist. The deep longing in marriage to find unity of heart, soul, and body should become a holy sphere and a holy will to be always ready to serve the other. With all his heart, the married partner must surrender his whole life to his beloved and be faithful in the objective covenant given by God. Thus the physical relationship is also holy. The holiness of marriage shows itself in this, that God himself is the Keeper of the bond between husband and wife. He is the Originator of the sexual relationship between one man and one woman. It is nothing to be ashamed of. It is only too holy to be constantly talked about. God rejoices in it when it comes under His rule; outside of His rule, it is sin.

How does this transformation of the sexual sphere take place? Love can transform life into a fruitful community of the Spirit. The Spirit has the strength and the power to transform everything in our hearts. Let us think of Pentecost. What happened then? The Spirit came. The Spirit is love, and this love was able to transform thousands so that their hearts melted like wax. They burned for Christ and were willing to die for Him as Stephen did. No human power can bring such a change about that thousands of people are of one heart and one soul. You can try it with your own will or coerce others with your will, but the only result is a terrible dictatorship. The will that effects a true change can be born only through a movement of heart and spirit from within.

With our own will we can certainly try to free ourselves from envy, for instance, and we may be able to overcome this envy to a certain degree. But with our own will we will never be able to overcome it completely in our hearts. Love alone can dissolve it, melt it away. Love is the only power that can overcome the evil of this world, and therefore it says in the New Testament: God is Love. We may be able to make a great effort to jump over our emotional feelings, but we will never be able to bring about the atmosphere in which two hearts become one. Only the Holy Spirit can do this, uniting people to become of one heart, one mind, and one soul. However hard we try, as long as it is only our *will* to be united with our partner and nothing happens in our *heart,* as long as the act of uniting in marriage is

Marriage in the Holy Spirit

carried only by our good will toward our partner, it remains a foreign body to the Spirit.

Many married couples in the world live in sexual relationship and are faithful without the Holy Spirit, and that may not be sin, but it is not organic, it is something ultimately brutal; it touches the sphere of the heart and spirit of another person without the deep, tender love of the Spirit, and because of that there is something animal in it. If two people unite only for a certain purpose, for instance to create new life, without inner unity of heart and soul, the unity is not as God wants it.

Love is the wonderful secret. Love owns the possibility of bringing about an experience that changes a man's life; it forms an area in which the material world is transformed into something divine. I want to bring Pentecost to mind again. When the Holy Spirit came, first people's hearts were struck, they repented and were baptized, and then the material world was affected. *The material became something holy.* The Spirit rejoices in penetrating the material world! All goods were collected, sold, and the proceeds laid at the Apostles' feet. Everyone wanted to give all they had out of love. There was no law about it. Not even Jesus had said exactly how it should be done, as far as we know; it is not recorded anywhere. He had said, "Sell all you have, give it to the poor." At Pentecost it just happened: the Spirit united hearts and it affected the physical sphere. So no one suffered need anymore; everyone received his share.

We have to be watchful that the material world does not rule us. The Spirit must rule the material world. We have to let the Holy Spirit transform the practical, material, and economic world. That begins by sharing what we have with everyone who is called to a life of brotherhood or with anyone in need, if we know about it, whether he is a believer or an unbeliever. We cannot eat and let our neighbor starve. The dollar has no right to rule over us. I want to warn everybody again and again that this can happen. Living in community does not make us immune to it. I am very much afraid of the power of Mammon, of our making it too comfortable for ourselves. The way of the Spirit is very simple, and we want to be transformed *in every area of life* to find this simplicity. Mammonism is the cold rulership of the material world over the spirit. Jesus spoke very sharply against mammonism: we cannot serve two masters.

This is true for every Christian community; and it is especially true for marriage: marriage is the symbol of Christian community. If we let our hearts be changed by God, by God's Holy Spirit, then our practical, our material life is affected; it belongs to the material world that two people become of one flesh. We stand before the fact that our bodies,

Marriage in the Holy Spirit

which are something material, are created by God in such a way that they long to be melted together as one flesh in marriage. But our bodies must not take over; not even our good will must take over. God has to take over. He is the Creator of the body and He rejoices in marriage. Therefore there is no need to be fearful. What matters is whether our life is really given to God, and this is true for every part of life, spiritual, emotional, and physical. In our present time, the physical life rules in a special way, the dollar rules, Mammon rules, and sex is cut off from God. And sex cut off from God is fornication, it is sin.

The sensuous sphere has the special task of letting the Spirit of Jesus rule in the sensate and material world. This rulership should be over our whole life, whether we are married or not. But only a married life in which two hearts and two spirits are bound together in one Spirit can enter the sexual sphere with God's blessing. Wedded love has the key to open the door so that sensuality is transformed and God's joy and blessing rest on it. In true marriage the act of marital relationship is ruled no longer only by the will but by the love that binds both people together, since it is the specific expression and fulfillment of wedded love. Insofar as marriage is *love,* it begins in the inner man and finds an expression and specific fulfillment in the sexual sphere. Insofar as it is *wedded love*, this love will build up the marital community between two people in an organic way. Only love can transfigure the sexual sphere in such a wonderful way that both partners are overwhelmed by it.

It is the Spirit of God who overcomes the danger of being swallowed up by the purely sexual or sensual sphere or of building a marriage only on good will. In itself, the will is not in a position to avoid being swallowed up by the sensual sphere. Only the Spirit of Jesus can do this. The danger of being swallowed up by sensuality cannot be overcome unless we allow ourselves to be gripped, to be re-formed. Only the love that has a central place in our lives makes it possible for two people to become of one flesh in real purity. Only love can rule over man's heart, soul, and emotions, and over his body. Only the Holy Spirit holds this sovereignty and brings God's blessing in the most sensuous moments. It is in the nature of God's love to bring a married couple together in the sexual sphere. Love in the Holy Spirit does not act as if she would merely stand by but touches the hearts of both married partners and rules over the physical expression of marriage. It belongs to love to have power over this most important materialization of the sphere of the spirit, which is shown in marriage.

It is of utmost importance that the partners allow

their love to each other to be explicitly under the love of God. Unless man's spirit holds firmly to God, the waves of sensuality will break over his head. Being consciously anchored in God is the only decisive protection from the danger of being overcome by the sensual or by the material world. When our hearts are thus anchored in God, we know with certainty that we may experience the act of becoming one flesh under God's express blessing. We are assured in our inner hearts of His permission to lift the veil of the sexual area. Only in the awareness that God blesses marriage can husband and wife give themselves fully to this act of marriage. God can shape everything material as He wishes, and it is God alone who can take away these obstinate powers of the sensate world so that He alone rules over it.

What has been said about the danger of the material world gaining power is true of the danger of being swallowed up by the emotions of sensuality, the danger of throwing oneself away. Our will is not strong enough to overcome this danger, which exists wherever true wedded love is not found. It may be that a partner gives himself or herself to the other out of a feeling of duty and respect. Then in the eyes of God he may not be throwing himself away, and God may even sanction such an act of surrender. But the need for a real transformation is not overcome. By giving ourselves to an experience of the sensual world without the rulership of God's love we are still in danger of throwing ourselves away. Even where for some reason the first love of marriage has grown cold, love is the only answer, love alone can bring about a change.

Let us consider a marriage in which only one of the partners is fully open to the love of God and the Holy Spirit, which awakens love from soul to soul and ultimately leads to becoming one flesh in marriage. It is a great need for the one partner that the heart of the other is not melted before God like wax. The only help is to lay this need before the Church by sharing it in a personal talk and then wait and pray. God opens doors. The Holy Spirit kindles flames. This blessing can also be given to a marriage that has lost something in the eyes of God, of which one partner is painfully aware. In this sense the suffering partner can give himself to the act of becoming one flesh. It is, then, a so-called giving oneself, submitting oneself, and so this act becomes the will to unite in wedded love.

This love between husband and wife that enables them to become of one heart and one soul is the only fulfillment of love in marriage. It is God's love, the love to do good. This alone brings a true, inner, and purposeful expression to the marriage so that neither partner loses himself in a wrong or superficial way. He does not throw himself away but gives

Marriage in the Holy Spirit

himself in the fear of God to the other, once and for all, until death parts them.

Especially in marriage, in order to be a true image of God each has to find a relationship *in God* to the other person. If the act of marital unity is bound absolutely *to God,* then it is an act of the most wonderful surrender. In a true marriage this is possible only as long as we are in God. If we forget God, if we continue to live in unlimited surrender to the beloved one without a close relationship to God, we throw ourselves into the gutter in a very deep way. This relationship to God in Jesus Christ and the love to Him comes through the Holy Spirit. Only in God and His Holy Spirit are we allowed to give ourselves completely to one another. Jesus says, *"Only he who loses his life will find it."* He is speaking of total surrender *to God,* but *in God* man can and should give himself to his fellowmen too.

Jesus says, "He who sins is a slave of sin." We are not free unless we are freed by God. Very many people who do not want to sin think they can achieve freedom by different methods, but without God and without Christ they will remain slaves.

Our surrender, then, has to be first a dedication to God, and in this dedication to God the right love to our neighbor will be given. Then every self-willed choice is impossible. From then on every choice is dependent on God. All capricious actions and all forms of superficiality have to be given up. All this inner disorder does not belong to the rulership of God. Only as long as man is in God is a true life possible. Instantly, at the same moment in which we give up God and do not put Him above everything, the order of the inner life is disturbed and man's *inner instinct is in need*.

This inner instinct is inborn in us. Every man has an instinct for what is good and what is not good. If we are not absolutely surrendered to God, this instinct does not react reliably anymore. It still reacts, but it is not reliable. My father, Eberhard Arnold, spoke often to us about the instinct of the Holy Spirit. That is a very special gift. It is not given to everyone in the Church in the measure he hoped it would be, in that it would be instinctively noticed if someone went wrong, not in the sense of mistrust but just out of love to that person; then the Holy Spirit would tell us through our instinct that there was something wrong so that we could help our brother.

The instinct of the Holy Spirit is especially needed in mission. When we stand in front of a group of people, our inner instinct should tell us what to say and what to be silent about, what would be unfitting to say in that circle. If this instinct does not give us a clear leading, we are in great danger of throwing pearls before swine. I think this instinct is in every

Marriage in the Holy Spirit

one of us to some degree, but in his last years my father said quite often that it needs to become stronger.

This instinct is needed in a special way for the marriage act, a shaking experience that is highly dramatic, an act of total surrender. Here the anchorage in God becomes a reality—the inner disorder is overcome by the feeling of responsibility under God's countenance. We look upward to God, whose love is endless. We will never be able to live out His full love, but we are able to make this love the center of our marriage. And that leads us to a holy, united love.

God gives us strength so that not even in thought and much less in deed do we do anything to harm the purity of our relationship as true Christians. When with inner reverence and with God's sanction man steps on the holy ground of sexuality, his soul is given the humble beauty of inner redemption and freedom. In this freedom our love will be transfigured, and the reality of marriage will become full of beauty. If love in marriage is anchored in God, the saying becomes true, "Love covers a multitude of sins." That is a very deep word. We should never forget it. Whenever we do a deed of love, when we really love, it has a healing effect on ourselves too if we do not think of ourselves. If we think of ourselves, it is not true love. If we forget ourselves in love, it covers a multitude of sins.

In the Beatitudes our Lord Jesus Christ praises purity of heart. The pure in heart shall see God. To the pure in heart God's final goal for all men will be revealed in a special way. They shall see God the Eternal in ineffable beauty, beyond our imagination. Something of this we experience in our life even though no man has ever seen God the Father. Yet through Jesus Christ and His Spirit something is revealed to men. Therefore it can hardly be expressed strongly enough what an abomination it is before God to take away the veil of sexuality for any other purpose than that for which God created it.

15. THE GLORY OF PURITY

Up to this point we have seen more the great dangers to a pure heart if it is not led by the instinct of the Holy Spirit. Now we want to concern ourselves with the positive unfolding of the glory of purity in marriage, the blessedness of purity. The main purpose for which the sexual sphere is created is not purity in itself, as we have seen, but surrendered love and the deep mystery of unity. The miracle is that this act of sensuous and sexual unity can take place in complete purity. The essence and mystery of love, of faithfulness, and of goodness is unity. In love God reveals Himself as Lord of unity.

How must the truly pure in heart experience this sphere so that they never for a moment turn from the countenance of God—so that they experience pure joy? In such joy the pure in heart can shine before God. I do not mean that we should constantly think in religious terms. We are speaking about a much greater reality. When we do not think in religious terms of God and Christ but love our brothers, then this reality is there. This is also true in marriage. We should never feel forced into a religious straightjacket. It is possible to talk as brothers about quite mundane things, like taking children on an outing. We can do this in the sight of God without mentioning His name or thinking of Him at that moment. If our marriages and our whole lives are under God, He is simply there.

There are people who have a deep will toward unity and purity, but whose natures are impure. Not only are they exposed to the specific temptations that attack modern man, but their whole natural inclination is toward the sexual sphere as an end in itself, which is what makes a man impure. In spite of all this he can in reality *want* full purity, if he *wants* to be free from any willful act of impurity. The will, which in Christ would bring a full transformation, does not yet rule over the whole person. What is necessary here is the baptism of the Holy Spirit—rebirth—which comes through repentance, conversion, and faith. Many people in our time have yet to find the freedom of a heart that is not chained to evil lust. Because of this, they can get very depressed by all the impure thoughts that belong to the sensual world independent of God (the world of sex for its own sake).

Here it is necessary to realize that there are different grades of purity. A man stands at the first grade

The Glory of Purity

of purity if his deeds are pure and his will is pure even if his whole nature is not yet pure. He does not yet carry the virtue of purity consistently throughout his life or radiate purity. If the atmosphere of purity so pervades a person that it is part of his natural makeup, he has reached a second, much higher level of purity. His mind is not occupied with the isolated sphere of the sensual pleasure—neither evil lust nor the special charm of impurity that attracts some people. He will avoid any situation or way of life that brings a danger in this direction. Neither seeking after it nor delighting in it comes up in his heart. True, he may sometimes have temptations in the area of sex for its own sake, but these will be exceptions. Deep in his heart there is such a complete rejection of anything impure that his whole attitude is one of distaste for the impurity of our time. He becomes pure. His whole being is so deeply imbedded in purity that if he meets anything impure it is nothing but an abomination and a pain for him. He avoids any place where he feels the intoxicating and oppressive atmosphere of fleshly lust. The direction of his thoughts is such that as a rule he would not even think of this area. This is the virtue of purity.

Here I want to say a special word for those of our young people who go out to high school and college; they are just as temptable as young people anywhere.

We live in a sick age. Young people talk of sex revolution and mean license to do whatever they please. It must be hard to imagine how our young people can go to high school and college and live a pure life in our time. Impurity is not to be seen everywhere in the same crude way, but they feel a real disgust at the intoxicating, oppressive atmosphere of sheer lust. Impurity often shows itself in such an ugly and repulsive way that it is practically no temptation anymore. To be almost immune to temptation is a gift in itself. We must not lose courage if we are temptable. Jesus was tempted in the wilderness. We can strive for the purity that protects us in temptation. "Blessed is the man who stands firm in temptation." It is the deepest will of the heart that counts—the very deepest will, which we meet in ourselves only in hours of quiet before God.

To the person who is given the third grade of purity God has given special grace. He represents God's innocence and God's purity on this polluted earth. He responds to the positive side of the sexual sphere in marriage, but if sex becomes an end in itself, he is not open to it; it is an abomination to him. There are people who become completely one with Jesus.

People with this highest degree of God-given purity have a special, divine love. Their openness to the sensuous and sexual sphere is filled to such a

The Glory of Purity

degree with God's love that it can assert itself only in the presence of God. They go through the world unsullied by the sin in the world. Impurity does not tempt them. This purity is not inborn; it is a gift from God. Such men and women are by natural disposition open to marriage, but they allow the veil of sexuality to be lifted only when they are sure that it is God's will. This is a special grace, a grace of rebirth, a grace that comes only from a complete surrender to God. It is of greatest importance that our will is absolutely decided for what is pure so that everything impure is rejected right from the beginning. If our surrender to God is firm in the area of purity, this grace of God can remain in us. But as soon as we become lame and lukewarm, we lose God, and then we have not far to go before we fall prey to sexual fascination, and evil lust takes over.

If we look at the attitude of a man who has experienced the grace of rebirth and is completely surrendered to God, we find that the sensuous sphere in marriage attracts him only by its tender intimacy. Here the uniting and melting together of two such surrendered people is truly blessed by God. There is nothing of intoxicating lust, yet that does not exclude joy in the physical sphere because the whole experience is carried also by the soul, and the soul is under the leadership of God's Spirit. The deep reverence of the pure man and his shyness before the solely physical—or looking *only* at that—lead to a deep understanding between husband and wife and strengthen their attitude of shunning the isolated physical sphere. Fulfillment is love from heart to heart in the knowledge of God's blessing.

The pure man therefore experiences to the depths of his being the serious and binding nature of the act of becoming one flesh. To the one who is pure, the physical act does not become secondary—it becomes the most noble joy. As soon as this speaking (even without words) of heart to heart and soul to soul comes to an end, the uniting of two souls loses all its joy, and marriage becomes a heavy duty.

To understand how the sexual sphere is transfigured in the life of a pure man, we must look at the part intimate tenderness plays in a true marriage. The love of a married couple must be full of tenderness in relationship to the act of physical uniting. This tenderness, this gentleness and love full of mercy, transfigures the whole act. In our time we have to warn that petting is not to be confused with this kind of tenderness. Petting between unmarried people as it is known today is completely divorced from God.

The urge to do good to the beloved is one of the basic elements of love. Tenderness in the intimacy of marriage is one expression of it. It becomes the

The Glory of Purity

greatest protection against naked lust and has a healing quality. It can never appear isolated but is always the expression of true love, an outpouring from the heart of one partner to the other.

The element of married love we just spoke about is the will to do good to the married partner. Another basic element is the urge and longing for uniting. Both are necessary in a true marriage and both have to be under the blessing of God. Both need a response from the other partner, which must be an outpouring of goodness and love to the beloved. It means a complete Yes, a wish to surrender one's heart to the other and a longing for uniting. It brings a longing for the heart of the other. The wish to belong completely to the other, to become one with him, is a living experience. It is a longing to take part in the very being of the other. All this must be completely under Jesus. If we find gentleness through Jesus, we will find a deep humility, first toward Jesus and then toward our partner. This love will bring a true and new relationship and provides an answer to many things in life.

I want to say here to all those who are not married that both elements of love should rule our whole community life—the longing to do good to our neighbor, that is, to do good for God's sake, to do the will of God; and the longing for unity, which is the strongest element in our love to God. To do God's will is the way to show our love to Him. In this sense we give our whole lives in love. The longing for uniting is the main purpose of our life in brotherhood. Even if we are married, our will to do good and our longing for uniting should be stronger toward the community and toward God than toward each other in marriage. In the love of a mother, the urge to do good is the most important factor. In marriage and in our relationship to God, the longing for unity is the strongest factor. In our Brotherhood, both have to become stronger—the urge to do good, that is, to do God's will, and the longing for unity. And if we love God, we long for this for all men. A passion to get married, a longing to possess someone else, is not love. Love is willing to give. Love is willing to renounce anything not given by God.

Tenderness is a way to seek the heart of the other. The partner wants to reach out; he wants to pour out his love through goodness. Tenderness, like caressing or embracing, may not seem so important, but it is a direct way to do good and show love. The crown of tenderness is the kiss. It seeks a uniting. It is an expression of all love—not only of husband and wife but of parents and children, of brother to brother and sister to sister, or of grown-ups to children.

We want in no way to say that the ideal purity of marriage allows only tenderness and no sensuousness.

The Glory of Purity

The opposite is the case: sensuousness in its unique intimacy is of greatest importance for the uniting of two partners. But tenderness and showing love to the other must come before the becoming of one flesh, which is meant by God as an expression of love and the longing to become of one heart, soul, and body.

16. MARRIAGE IN THE CHURCH

The task of woman is different from that of man. That is clear from the story of the creation: how man was created and how woman was taken from man. In the New Testament both Paul and Peter point out that man is the head of woman. Paul likens marriage to Christ and His Church, comparing man to Christ and woman to the Church. It is not a question of who is *higher*, man or woman. Both are made in the image of God, and what can be greater than that? The fact that woman was taken from man and man is born of woman shows that they are dependent on each other in every respect.

Yet in a true marriage the husband gives the lead. At a wedding in the Hutterian Church the bridegroom is asked if he is willing to lead his wife to everything that is good, which means to lead her deeper and deeper to Jesus, and the bride is asked if she is willing to follow her husband in everything that is good. Next comes the decisive question of the Church, whether husband and wife are willing to put Christ and His Church above the covenant of marriage: if one of them experiences the shipwreck of his faith and leaves the life of discipleship, will the other put loyalty to Christ and the Church above loyalty to marriage?

For this reason no baptized member of the Hutterian Church may marry someone of a different faith or an unbeliever. It would be in contradiction to our belief in the unity of spirit and faith as the first grade in marriage. Should someone who is married to an unbeliever or someone of a different belief wish to join the Church, the Church would go a long way to save this marriage as long as the latter does not hinder the member of the Church in his faith and in participating in the life of the community.

> To the rest I say this, as my own word, not as the Lord's: if a Christian has a heathen wife, and she is willing to live with him, he must not divorce her; and a woman who has a heathen husband willing to live with her must not divorce her husband. For the heathen husband now belongs to God through his Christian wife, and the heathen wife through her Christian husband. Otherwise your children would not belong to God, whereas in fact they do. If on the other hand the heathen partner wishes for a separation, let him have it. In such cases the Christian husband or wife is under no compulsion; but God's call is a call to

live in peace. Think of it: as a wife you may be your husband's salvation; as a husband you may be your wife's salvation. (1 Cor. 7:12–16, NEB)

In the same way as Christ is the Head of His Church, the husband should be the head of his wife. The Head who illuminates everything, being Bearer of the Spirit, is the Bearer of light for the whole world, and this light shall shine for all men. This Head who is the Light-Bearer wants the Father's will to be revealed "so that, when they see the good you do, they may give praise to your Father in heaven." (Matt. 5:16, NEB)

God's breath is the breath of life blowing directly from Him *now*. It is not a matter of repeating words spoken by Him in the past. The breath of God—the Word that comes to us directly from God—is revealed now. Jesus says, " 'Full authority in heaven and on earth has been committed to me. Go forth therefore and make all nations my disciples; baptize men everywhere in the name of the Father and the Son and the Holy Spirit, and teach them to observe all that I have commanded you. And be assured, I am with you always, to the end of time.' " (Matt. 28:18–20, NEB) This is the spiritual authority of the Head, who is often understood as the Redeemer who forgives sin but seldom as the Teacher who reveals the truth.

In the example of Mary we recognize the true nature of woman. In the example of the apostle we recognize man and his task. His is the apostolic task: "Go out and gather! Teach all people. Submerge them in the atmosphere of God, in the life of God the Father, the Son, and the Holy Spirit." It is the apostle's task to lead to the obedience of faith. This is the task of a word leader. It is the task of the husband for his wife and children. The husband represents Christ as the Head, even if he is a very weak person. It is the task of teachers, both men and women, and of the sisters who work with smaller children. Women are in no way excluded from this task in its innermost sense, but it is in a special way the task of the apostolic man.

The head, the word leader, has to represent the Word, which is Christ. That must not be taken as if man were the overlord. It must be accepted deeply in the atmosphere of the Spirit. Otherwise something quite terrible happens. But in the true Church, under the leading of the Holy Spirit, it will become something God-given. Then Christ can come into His own.

Whenever we wish to show our love, we wish to show it in the flesh, which is the active instrument of the soul. The body cannot love; we cannot love with the body. The only way of truly loving is with our innermost heart, soul, and being. The more deeply

Marriage in the Church

we experience the love of Jesus Christ and love to Jesus Christ, the more fully will we experience love in engagement and marriage. The body is made to give expression to the impulses of the heart. A gentle smile, eyes that shine from an affectionate word, or a tender touch of the hand can lead to an ardent embrace and caresses of final fulfillment in union. The body is the soul made visible. Also, the more complete our spiritual surrender to the beloved, the more harmonious will be our physical surrender. As soon as a young couple is married, they are allowed to come so close to each other that they find complete physical unity. Here the physical side of love is protected by modesty and by reverence for the body of the other. Chastity in marriage rests on consideration for the dignity of one's own body as much as for that of the other. Egoism and selfishness destroy love.

The woman longs to absorb her beloved into herself. The man desires to enter into her and become one with her. He is creative by nature, made to take and penetrate rather than to give. In this lies the characteristic difference between man and woman. The woman is by nature designed to give, to endure, to conceive, to bear, to nurse, and to protect. It belongs to the evil nature of our time that woman revolts against carrying the burden and pain of pregnancy and birth. Her nature was designed by

God, and especially in this area no irreverent talking should be tolerated. A true man who carries his own burdens respects and loves his wife all the more when she bears him children in pain and labor.

In the sphere of love, the determining factor is always the nonphysical. The determining factor must be the relationship from heart to heart and from soul to soul out of love to Jesus. Therefore we must not forget that for us the body without the soul is merely the form of man, only matter. Yet we should not despise it on that account. " 'Do you not know that your body is a shrine of the indwelling Holy Spirit, and the Spirit is God's gift to you?' " (Cor. 6:19, NEB) It has been said that man is a body shaped by a soul. I believe these are deep words, but we should not forget that man's spirit or soul is breathed by God into his body. The shaping of the body comes from God. Therefore, because the soul shapes the body, there are differences in the biological makeup of male and female. But it is completely materialistic to think that the difference between man and woman is mainly biological. It is the opposite. The soul, the innermost essence of man and woman, forms a different body for each, or better expressed, God did it by breathing His breath into them.

I do not want to go into the physical differences between men and women and the physical side of marriage. I want to make only one point: marriage must be ruled by love. Love demands that we take care of the beloved one. Firstly, the woman is the weaker one, and therefore the husband in his love should take the attitude of sheltering her. Secondly, he should know that the woman reacts more slowly in the area of sex than the man. She needs time until she is ready for the act of becoming one flesh. Much patience, tenderness, and love is needed until each partner knows the other. How often does it happen that the young husband falls happily asleep while his young wife lies awake a long time in a certain emptiness, unfulfilled longing, and inner need. Because of this the husband should have strong self-control, and his love to his wife should lead him to wait till the right hour for physical union is given.

Finally I want to quote from the First Letter of Peter:

> Thus it was among God's people in days of old: the women who fixed their hopes on him adorned themselves by submission to their husbands. Such was Sarah, who obeyed Abraham and called him 'my master'. Her children you have now become, if you do good and show no fear.
>
> In the same way, you husbands must conduct your married life with understanding: pay honor to the woman's body, not only because it is weaker, but also because you share together in the grace of God which gives you life. Then your prayers will not be hindered. (1 Peter 3:5–7, NEB)

If a married couple take these words of the Apostle Peter really to heart and experience a true inner relationship—an inner speaking of the heart to God from both together—then God's blessing will be on their marriage.

17. ESPECIALLY FOR YOUNG COUPLES

We should consider what a high place marriage has in the Bible. We find it in the story of the creation, in the Ten Commandments, and in the New Testament: Jesus speaks of a man leaving father and mother and becoming one flesh with his wife. For young people growing up today, however, the whole area of marriage is terribly distorted. There is a very false idea that a new little life comes into being through something merely physical or biological. The mystery about the creation of a human being, a mystery no doctor or psychologist can describe, is forgotten today.

We know what it means to have one's first child, to see him smile for the first time, to love him and feel his love for us. We know that this child (who is only once on this earth) is like no other child. No other child can replace him in the hearts of his parents. Then if we experience the pain of losing this child, of seeing him die as he looks from father to mother and from mother to father to show his love with the last strength of his little body—if we have experienced all this, then we feel something of the greatness of God and His nearness in this little baby, who was created by God and *not* by man.

Frederick von Gagern writes: "The responsibility of marriage stretches far beyond the narrow field of the family.... How many of us perceive clearly the difference between sentimental substitutes for feeling and the real thing, which comes from the heart: between an outward appearance and the passionate devotion and concentrated will of loving souls able to forget themselves for the sake of each other"[1]— that is, to find unity of heart and soul through the Spirit of God? To be a living part in the greater community of the united Church as a married couple or as a family can be a very great experience. It is Jesus who gives it all to man's heart.

In our time especially it is important "to do justice to the inward vision of the human soul. Conclusions formed in general terms, and not with reference to this or that *specific* man or woman, will inevitably seem clumsy and inadequate—hardly more, in fact, than shadowy indications of the underlying reality. Nor can they claim to be all-inclusive or thorough. The ultimate things cannot be put into words. They

[1] All material quoted in this chapter is taken from Frederick von Gagern, M.D. *Difficulties in Married Life,* English translation by Meyrick Booth (New York: Paulist Press, 1964).

Especially for Young Couples

remain secret and mysterious." Nevertheless we want to speak about them in this book.

If one has had the opportunity of experiencing the birth of one's own child and of standing at the bedside of a dying person, one thing stands out: God alone counts at such moments—really *only* God. Today there is a very great inner need in young people. Many have turned away from the true God. For inner help they turn to psychology, which mostly treats man as an animal, and some throw themselves into politics. True, there are movements among young people who seek on a deeper and more serious level, who really seek the good. And yet the deep mystery of man's soul as the image of God is mocked publicly in schools and universities. "Even in the Middle Ages, St. Francis felt called upon to preach a renewal .... Since then, we have witnessed unceasing calls for reform and for a deepening of faith." In Germany and Switzerland there was the Reformation. One outcome of this was the founding of the Hutterian Church by the apostolic martyr Jakob Hutter, followed by the apostolic Word Leader Peter Rideman and the Anabaptist martyrs (more than two thousand) who died for the sake of divine truth, the truth of Jesus Christ. In England it was the Quaker movement through which God called men. The need for renewal was felt because of secularization on the one hand and rigid legalism leading to spiritual death on the other. In the nineteenth century "the working-classes fell before the anti-religious spirit and nowadays in the twentieth century, it would appear that the peasantry [in Europe], so long a firm pillar of faith, have become 'ripe' for withdrawal from God, and the cult of self-glorifying materialism." To see man divorced from God is to see the most terrible idolatry and self-glorification, which will bring God's judgment over our age. But let us ask God that in His compassion He opens ways for His warm light to shine into this corrupt generation. There is an inner emptiness. There is little sensitivity toward the Spirit. Men are actually lonely and forgotten.

"There are three main reasons for this: firstly, the insecurity and suffering into which our children are born are sufficient to awaken in us all the primordial fears and anxieties with which man is born." We only have to think of the weapons man has invented and how terribly murderous the spirit of our time is. Secondly, there is the very sad withdrawal from God, which creates a deep spiritual emptiness among young people. "This is a prime cause of mental and spiritual sickness, now so rapidly increasing.... Thirdly, the widespread and growing *lovelessness* of the modern world infects the souls of individuals, and undermines their capacity for love."

How can man find again the capacity to love? Of

Especially for Young Couples

primary importance is "a strong and genuine parental love giving the child security and freedom from anxiety, and laying the foundation of the capacity for love and dynamic faith." If we want our children to grow up in the right atmosphere, we have to help their hearts and characters to become firm and to stand up for the good. Today in high schools and on college campuses there is something at work that takes away their capacity to believe and to love.

How can the picture of modern society be changed so that a new life community is given, a life that is rightly ordered? We know in our Hutterian Bruderhof movement that the answer lies in faith alone. It has to start with repentance and conversion, which melt a man's heart like wax because he recognizes his own evil and the unending love of God. We cannot see any other solution for the millions of young people in America and Europe. And because of this we must rededicate our own lives so that God can do something, so that the salt in our life has real flavor, so that the City on the Hill has a real light, so that when we use the name of God, it comes from a heart of fire.

If we think of starting a family, the first question is: On what foundation? Complete dedication to Jesus and His Church is the foundation of everything. On this foundation—Jesus Christ—we are able to begin a rich and fulfilled married life and "create through such a marriage a bulwark protecting the new generation against spiritual need and disintegration and providing for it better opportunities than we enjoyed." If we want our children to experience fullness of life, we must make sure that our *marriages* come onto a true basis. Marriage is the soil in which the children grow—"if the soil is poor we cannot expect the flowers to be good."

It is of great importance to us that from his first day of life a child is surrounded by the love of God and by the fear of God. Fathers and mothers have the main responsibility for the education of their children. Only if fathers and mothers do their part can the Church and the educators plant and water that soil which is provided in the home. They can only support and strengthen the spiritual atmosphere that must come from the home. Yet I want to say a compassionate word to parents. Not all parents are equally gifted for educating their children. If gifts are lacking among us as parents, the Brotherhood will gladly step in and find ways to help so that the children are given the inner security they need.

There is no inner security for a child unless the commandments to honor father and mother, to fear God, and to love Him are kept. It is part of education to lead the child so that he experiences in

Especially for Young Couples

his little heart something of the greatness and goodness of God, the fear of God, and a real love to Jesus. This can be put into a child's heart so easily and simply by telling him about Jesus, from His birth in the stable at Bethlehem until His resurrection. All this moves the hearts of children even at a very young age. Parents and children must be helped to find the right attitude to life and to one another. There must be a working-together between parents, teachers, and the whole Brotherhood. The life of the Brotherhood and its Services on a Hutterian Bruderhof depends on hearts being confronted with God.

It is very important for children to learn the first commandment, to honor God; the fifth commandment, to honor father and mother; and the tenth commandment, not to covet. These should be laid on the heart of every child. But we should not plague little children with commandments they cannot understand or sins they cannot even commit, like adultery. Young people, however, should have a full knowledge of and a deep inner feeling for the Ten Commandments given to Moses. (I do not mean that they need to learn them by heart.)

God spoke, and these were his words:

I am the Lord your God who brought you out of Egypt, out of the land of slavery.

[1.] You shall have no other god to set against me.

[2.] You shall not make a carved image for yourself nor the likeness of anything in the heavens above, or on the earth below, or in the waters under the earth.

You shall not bow down to them or worship them; for I, the Lord your God, am a jealous god. I punish the children for the sins of the fathers to the third and fourth generations of those who hate me. But I keep faith with thousands, with those who love me and keep my commandments.

[3.] You shall not make wrong use of the name of the Lord your God: the Lord will not leave unpunished the man who misuses his name.

[4.] Remember to keep the sabbath day holy. You have six days to labour and do all your work. But the seventh day is a sabbath of the Lord your God; that day you shall not do any work, you, your son or your daughter, your slave or your slave-girl, your cattle or the alien within your gates; for in six days the Lord made heaven and earth, the sea, and all that is in them, and on the seventh day he rested. Therefore the Lord blessed the sabbath day and declared it holy.

[5.] Honour your father and your mother, that you may live long in the land which the Lord your God is giving you.

[6.] You shall not commit murder.

[7.] You shall not commit adultery.

[8.] You shall not steal.

Especially for Young Couples

[9.] You shall not give false evidence against your neighbour.

[10.] You shall not covet your neighbour's house; you shall not covet your neighbour's wife, his slave, his slave-girl, his ox, his ass, or anything that belongs to him. (Exodus 20:1–17, NEB)

Within the community of a Hutterian Bruderhof we know that we need a close working-together of parents and teachers, but how is it when our young people go out to high school and college? Von Gagern writes: "The harmonious relationship desired is destroyed as much by prudishness as it is by a materialistic biological approach." At the end of the last century, it was prudishness that damaged this relationship. Today it is an enormous shamelessness in the area of sex: we need not fear prudishness in high school. "Our aim is the preservation of natural reverence for the body and for sex, as given by God. From the point of view of marriage, the negative attitude of the sexually inhibited and the opposite extreme, recourse to sin, are equally opposed to what is right and healthy."

A child should acquire naturally, in his own home, a right attitude to his body and to sex. It should be the parents' privilege to teach their adolescent children and young people that the body is holy and that any defilement of it is a terrible sin. What is taught today is a horror—that there is no difference between the sex relationship of man and woman and that of animals. In my opinion it is very important for parents to tell their children that they must keep their bodies holy for the creative purpose of marriage. I well remember what a deep impression it made on my heart when my father went for a walk with me and told me about the struggle for a pure life, how to keep the body pure for the possibility of having children later. He also said to me, "If you manage *now* to live a pure life, it will be very easy later. If you give in now to impure passions, it will become harder and harder to withstand temptation later."

I believe it is not good to give a child too many biological facts about sex. It takes away too much of the mystery of birth and death. With this I do not mean taking a prudish attitude. I think his father or mother should speak with a child at the age of twelve, thirteen, or fourteen, when the time of adolescence begins. It is necessary that we call a spade a spade and are not afraid to talk freely in the right way about sex and the crime of abortion. Otherwise our children hear it talked about only in an evil atmosphere that makes it difficult for them to find the right attitude.

The instruction of young couples who want to be married is important, but I do not think that it

Especially for Young Couples

is necessary to know everything about sex before marriage. It is such a delicate area: it is something mysterious between husband and wife, and experience shows that it is good for them to find their own way together. Certainly some facts should be given. But how spirit, soul, and body find united expression in love should be the main concern. Young couples should have clear ideas about the holiness of marriage and the significance of love in marriage, but in actual fact *only love itself can show what is permissible and what is not.* Side by side with the direct approach, there should be an inner seeking in the gathered Church before a wedding to help young people find the right attitude to marriage. "The naivety with which many young people plunge into marriage is shocking! They do not understand the tasks imposed." I have heard that in California the life of very many young people is ruined in the sexual and marital sphere at the age of sixteen years or younger.

"Men and women with a serious sense of responsibility, however, who are contemplating marriage, or who are already married, examine the problems of marriage and the matter of educating children with care. They know that every profession requires preparation and none more than the vitally important one of marriage." The first and main thing is to build on Jesus and His commandments. "When a married couple realise that [they are no longer living on the basis of Jesus] ... renewed from day to day, or that their love is resting upon feet of clay, the time is more than ripe to make up for what has been lost and start afresh. Our first question accordingly, must be concerned with the *true nature* of love. How many people have long ago lost touch with even the meaning of the word!"

The love that leads to marriage has three stages. "When we meet another fellow-human, our first question is: 'Who are you—what sort of a man or woman are you?' We seek to penetrate the character, to get to know him or her." If we feel from the person we meet an atmosphere of purity and goodness that streams out and speaks to our inmost soul, "then there arises in ourselves a deep and happy satisfaction through harmony with this other human. It is then we feel moved to cry: 'I am filled with joy to see you, to know that you *exist*.'"

Then if we really feel in our hearts that this is the human being who is meant for us, if we feel it is Jesus who leads us together, we say with our hearts a joyful Yes! "Perhaps we feel compelled to communicate the flood of emotion that fills us, to a close friend, to whom we sing the praises of the beloved, or perhaps to God, to whom we cry: 'I thank Thee that Thou hast created this human being! He

Especially for Young Couples

is the revelation of Thy beauty and goodness. I feel that in him I find Thyself!' "

This is the moment when the united Brotherhood is called upon. The brother who feels such a love for a sister shares his feeling with a Servant of the Word.[1] From this moment on the relationship is under the Church. At the right time the Brotherhood will be asked whether the two may make a bond for life. From the beginning it is of chief importance that for both bride and bridegroom *Jesus and the Church are everything.* For Jesus we give our lives. He is greater than our love to each other.

When it is clear that Jesus is all in all, we can say: "Now we are no longer satisfied to gaze and wonder, to admire and to adore—we want to participate in this treasure, and yearn for mutual love, for that exchange of hearts which is expressed in giving and receiving, thus fulfilling itself."

The third step is more difficult, for it depends on the question: Are we willing to have a serving love? "We not only accept the value of the beloved one but set it as our aim to *increase this value.* 'I want you to be as good as is possible, as fulfilled, as rich, as happy as can be conceived! And what I can do to bring this about *shall* be done.' "

---

[1] The Servant of the Word has a special responsibility for the inner life of the Church and for bringing to expression the living Word of God given to the Church.

There is a big difference between love and love. The Greek language has several words for love, including *eros* and *agape*. A love that is only passionate will not endure. It is not enough that married couples experience only *eros,* the purely personal, emotional love to each other. They need *agape,* the serving, self-giving love.

> In every-day love it is the rule that we find the two first steps and indeed without these two pillars the house of love and marriage could not stand. But if the building is not to collapse with the first puff of wind, the third pillar, imparting stability to the whole, is essential. Yet this pillar is so often absent. Why? Because it is at this point that we have to overcome the inertia of our own hearts which so often tends to act as a brake. It is not just a question of a matter-of-fact effort of will which can come from the mind alone, but of a passionate heart-felt will. It is not a pious wish that is needed, not a mild good-will, but an ardent devotion to all that can further the fulfilment of the beloved. That is the ideal! How very far are most of us from attaining to it.

18. FATHERHOOD AND MOTHERHOOD

It is the task of married couples to bring up their children in God's stead since to their children father and mother represent the Creator. Children must honor father and mother. This should be imprinted on the heart of the very young child; it is actually alive in him already. In man there is a longing for God even before he is aware of it. For the small child, father and mother stand for God.

It is terrible when parents have only the outward appearance of being parents without really being father and mother to their children. Unfortunately many children grow up fatherless and motherless in their inner lives although they actually have a father and a mother. This will always be the case when parents fail in the task of helping their children in God's stead.

There is no doubt that a child looks to his parents for something of the security that we grown-ups can find only in community in and with God. Children easily become emotionally sick if parents do not fulfill this inner longing in them. There are family situations in which the father and mother live in dissension and the children cannot find a true picture of God the Creator. No wonder that later in life they have trouble mastering their insecurity in finding a real, living foundation that supports their lives as beings created by God. As his soul matures, a person ponders over and works out for himself what the true image of a father and the true image of a mother should be. In this process the individual really can find a foundation in Him who created him. When this happens, it is always grace at work.

This symbolic link between the concept of fatherhood and motherhood and that of God helps us to understand that it is hard for a person's concept of God to thrive in his heart unless he sees God's image in his parents. When this is lacking, the souls of the children suffer. For instance, when parents fail to let their God-given authority assert itself in an inner way from the depth of their hearts, when they use outward means and impose their greater power, perhaps in a hardhearted way—then they not only destroy the image of God but endanger their children. The children's souls and inner development are harmed and they can become emotionally sick.

Parents are mediators between the child and the world just as they are between the child and God.

Fatherhood and Motherhood

Where true love is missing and where parents, realizing their guilt or not, fail their children (perhaps because things are not right in their marriage), this image is missing and the consequences are terrible. Then the children fall into an abnormal inner attitude toward themselves, as von Gagern puts it. Without doubt an "abnormal inner attitude" is emotional sickness.

Parents are usually not as guilty for this as one assumes, for they do not intentionally mislead their children. Consciously or unconsciously, they themselves suffer for failing to win through either to the true concept of fatherhood and motherhood or to the image of God. In this day and age we can really say quite generally that the true concept of father and mother is lost. This whole generation is corrupt. When we look at the general development here in America and in Europe, we see that there is little honoring of father and mother anymore. It is really godless to raise children without respect for father and mother and without reverence for God.

This book therefore presents a challenge to all parents. They can find the image of God reflected in themselves by seeking it directly in prayer, by unburdening themselves to the Church, by steadfastly seeking to understand what God means by man being made in His image. They find their own divine image by finding the Father in Heaven in quite a new way. Christ shows us the image of God and, in doing so, a new man who has a likeness to the image of God. Therefore we should pray: "O God, Thou hast created man so wonderfully in his dignity, and Thou hast restored him to his dignity even more wonderfully." The possibility of finding God completely and so restoring God's image is given completely anew through the stable in Bethlehem and the Cross at Golgotha.

Therefore we have no excuse. When we take the bond of marriage upon ourselves, the husband is responsible for leading his wife to Christ. And the wife makes it her duty to be a true helper to her husband. She makes it her task to educate her children in the right fear of God.

19. THE SPECIAL SERVICE OF THE UNMARRIED AND THE WIDOWED

It is possible for everyone to find the deepest unity of heart and soul without marriage. The New Testament even indicates that a deeper dedication to Christ may be found by giving up marriage for the sake of the Kingdom of God than by entering into marriage. Jesus closes His words about giving up marriage by saying: "Let those accept it who can." (Matt. 19:12) These words of Jesus show the depth of the mystery connected with giving up marriage for the sake of the Kingdom of Heaven. They show us that there is a calling in the Church besides marriage. To remain single can lead to a very high calling if one is able to accept it deeply in one's heart. Those who give up everything, also the great gift of marriage, for Jesus, are given a great promise. Jesus is especially close to them and will be very near them at His coming.

> The disciples said to him, 'If that is the position with husband and wife, it is better not to marry.' To this he replied, 'That is something which not

everyone can accept, but only those for whom God has appointed it. For while some are incapable of marriage because they were born so, or were made so by men, there are others who have themselves renounced marriage for the sake of the kingdom of Heaven. Let those accept it who can.'
(Matt. 19: 10–12, NEB)

Widows, like the unmarried, are freer to serve than the married. Therefore some widows have a very deep calling to serve Jesus and the Church. "A widow, however, in the full sense, one who is alone in the world, has all her hope set on God, and regularly attends the meetings for prayer and worship night and day." (1 Tim. 5:5, NEB) In the early Church widows were appointed to serve the poor or to serve the Church community in a special way. They had the trust of the whole congregation. Eberhard Arnold, in his *Early Christians,* says, "In even the smallest Church community the overseer had to be a friend to the poor, and there had to be at least one widow responsible to see to it, day and night, that no sick or needy person was neglected."[1]

In early Church prophecy the word Church was understood in a much greater and deeper sense than it is today. How small the "Church of God" becomes

---

[1] Eberhard Arnold, *The Early Christians after the Death of the Apostles,* selected and edited from all the sources of the first centuries, 2nd ed. (Rifton, NY: Plough Publishing House, 1972), p. 18.

Service of Unmarried and Widowed

when one speaks of all the different sects and Churches as Church of Christ! How great God, His Christ, and His Holy Spirit become if we believe in the Church which was from the beginning and will be to all Eternity! In the prophecy called "The Shepherd of Hermas" that is very deeply expressed: "Because the Church was created before all other things, she is old. It was for her sake that the world was formed."[1]

The fact that some feel called to remain single for the sake of Jesus points to a special act of love and is a sign of an undivided heart. The Apostle Paul writes: "But those who marry will have pain and grief in this bodily life, and my aim is to spare you." (1 Cor. 7:28, NEB) He refers to the time of persecution. In our day this has to be taken very seriously. Old and New Testament prophecy foretells terrible days. It is our task to educate our children to be courageous. They must learn to take a stand for their convictions so that they do not fall into the hands of the Evil One in the horrors of the last days, especially in the very last days, the days of the Antichrist.

These are all reasons for giving up marriage. The undividedness with which a person gives up everything for Jesus brings about a special relationship to Him. Such a person suffers for the sake of Jesus because the soul wants to be like Him in all things. When someone decides to give up marriage for the sake of Jesus, it is a symbol of total dedication to

[1] Eberhard Arnold, *The Early Christians,* p. 278.

Him. He is always in the hands of Jesus in a special way. All men are challenged to a complete transformation in Christ: "That not we live but Christ in us." (Gal. 2:20) But this takes on a particular meaning for the one who is single or widowed and who carries his need for Christ's sake. The immersion in Christ symbolized in baptism is man's deepest calling. A life for Christ is life in its fullest sense. We learn to love Christ as the true Bridegroom. We also learn to love His children, our brothers and sisters.

For those who have had no chance to marry and who feel no special calling to remain single for the sake of Jesus there is a special danger that their hearts become hardened. Only grace can protect them from this danger. Special grace is needed for the single or widowed to forego all the earthly and heavenly gifts offered in marriage.

We must come to a deep encounter with Jesus Christ whether we are married or single. This is all-important. It is the theme of this whole book. We must ask God that we may see Jesus as He is. This is a very great gift. I think many have been touched by Jesus, have experienced something of Him, and have been called by Him, but we must ask God that we may see Jesus *as He is*. When a person uses many religious words, the question arises: Does he know what he is saying? All ideas about Jesus must die if they come out of our own hearts or minds and are

Service of Unmarried and Widowed

not in keeping with the truth. Then we will be overwhelmed by Him. If we want to speak about the husband being the head of his wife as Christ is the Head of His Church, we must ask God that it is given to us more fully to see Christ as He really is. Then the picture of Christ and His Church can in all humility be represented even if it is incomplete.

It is the special longing of my heart that as a Brotherhood we ask for this first of all for ourselves. Then we may represent Him in our time in everything—in marriage, in our relationship with other religious groups, and in our relationship with the world. Jesus came and said, "I came on earth to kindle a fire. How I wish it were already burning!" (Luke 12:49)

We have a very short span of life. The true picture of Jesus Christ as He is would be the greatest gift for our time. I think that the true picture of Jesus is not seen clearly enough today. Where is Jesus— as He was and is—most revealed? We must seek brothers. We must ask that Christ is revealed today. That is the salt of which Jesus speaks, that He is represented *as He is*: as full of tenderness, meekness, and humility as He is but also in all His sharpness. We must not add or take away anything.

This we wish for all young couples. When we ask for God's blessing for a young couple, we ask that Jesus may be revealed to us as He is. He is the Head of us all.

BIBLIOGRAPHY

Arnold, Eberhard. *Love and Marriage in the Spirit.* Rifton, NY: Plough Publishing House, 1965.

———. *The Early Christians after the Death of the Apostles.* 2nd ed. Rifton, NY: Plough Publishing House, 1972.

Arnold, Eberhard and Emmy. *Seeking for the Kingdom of God: Origins of the Bruderhof Communities.* Edited by Heini and Annemarie Arnold. Rifton, NY: Plough Publishing House, 1974.

Gagern, Friedrich E. Freiherr v. *Mann und Frau: Einführung in das Geheimnis der Ehe.* Frankfurt am Main: Verlag Josef Knecht, 1953.

———. *Der Mensch als Bild: Beiträge zur Anthropologie.* 2nd ed. Frankfurt am Main: Verlag Josef Knecht, 1955.

———. *Difficulties in Married Life.* Translated by Meyrick Booth. New York: Paulist Press, 1964.

Hildebrand, Dietrich v. *Reinheit und Jungfräulichkeit*. Zürich: Benziger Verlag, 1950.

Rideman, Peter. *Confession of Faith: Account of Our Religion, Doctrine, and Faith*. Originally published in 1545 as *Rechenschaft unserer Religion, Lehr und Glaubens, von den Brüdern, so man die Hutterischen nennt, ausgangen durch Peter Rideman*. Translated by the Hutterian Society of Brothers. 2nd ed. Rifton, NY: Plough Publishing House, 1970.